POLITICAL
SOLIDARITY
ECONOMY

JORGE SANTIAGO
SANTIAGO

POLITICAL SOLIDARITY ECONOMY

JORGE SANTIAGO
SANTIAGO

This book is the translated, modified English version of the book *Economia Politica Solidaria: Construyendo Alternativas* published in Mexico, in 2019. This book was published with the support of Social Economic Development of Indigenous Mexicans (DESMI) and sponsored by Thousand Currents (Miles de Afluentes). The views and opinions expressed in this book are those of the author and do not necessarily reflect the views and opinions of Thousand Currents.

Political Solidarity Economy

Published by Gatekeeper Press
2167 Stringtown Rd, Suite 109
Columbus, OH 43123-2989
www.GatekeeperPress.com

Publication Coordination: Mónica Carrillo Zegarra
Translation: Sayra Pinto, Ximena Izquierdo Ugaz, Jamie San Andrés
Copy editors: Jamie San Andrés, David Pastor
Exterior and Interior Design: Camila Bustamante

Library of Congress Control Number: TBD

ISBN (paperback): 9781662918049
eISBN: 9781662918056

Contents

Prologue

ASSEMBLING MANY YEARS OF JORGE SANTIAGO SANTIAGO'S WORK, REFLECTIONS, AND DIALOGUES, we bring you this book titled *Political Solidarity Economy*, as a preamble to Social Economic Development of Indigenous Mexicans' (DESMI's) 50th anniversary celebration, commemorating our path and our work.

Political Solidarity Economy seeks to generate debate, reflection, and act as a resource for all of us individuals, communities, and organizations who work, care for, and construct alternatives of living alongside our people in hope of forging another economy.

Political Solidarity Economy is grounded in collective work, as well as care and respect towards Mother Earth. This collective work is strengthened through agroecological work, women's participation, and the practice of mutual dialogue. Solidarity political economy also means creating collectives that are spaces for sharing knowledge and recovering customs dating back thousands of years; generating autonomous communal structures; and helping us to raise consciousness in the face of dispossession that threatens our territories now more than ever.

Whether we call it social economy or social and solidarity economy, in *Political Solidarity Economy*, Jorge provides us with the elements needed for a global vision of reality, as a call to understand and discover the relationships of production in an economic system that is based on dispossession and exploitation. Therefore, understanding the means of production and the distribution of goods is a political act in the sense that we want to be collective subjects for change.

Concepts, strategies and practices must go hand in hand. Agroecology is not possible without a political solidarity economy. There cannot be agroecology without political solidarity economy, and none of this can exist if we do not defend our land and territory. There must be self-determination and a struggle for these things—that is why we see the need for the system's radical transformation.

This book is an invitation to deepen our reflections about collectivity. The intention of our end goal is not market solidarity, the promotion of exchanges, or the formation of cooperatives or collectives for production, but rather that these alternatives seek to conserve the lives of Mother Earth's people, and become the engine for transformation that brings us into the work and struggle for our peoples' autonomy.

María Estela Barco Huerta

DESMI, A.C. Coordinator

Holding Space

Foreword

THIS BOOK IS A HARMONIOUS AND LOGICAL CONSTRUCTION THAT TAKES INTO ACCOUNT FORWARD THINKING DESIRES, INTUITIONS, AND PERSPECTIVES.

It seeks to achieve a globally structured perspective that privileges historical processes and the historical construction of social subjects searching for change and for a new social model that emerges from balancing humanity and nature, while highlighting the elements that act as seeds of this new reality and paradigm.

Solidarity economy is seen as the global construction of new relationships that make possible coexistence, creativity, and the equitable distribution of goods, so that we may enjoy time and space to be free, and build a house where all are welcome. This line of thought aligns with the Ejercito Zapatista de Liberación Nacional (EZLN)'s proposal for autonomy and peoples' rights—not as charity but as a self-determined construction.

Solidarity economy must be understood from a global vision of mutual support, land, knowledge, and an understanding of the power of orality. This, in turn, generates autonomous practices, or if you will, alternative practices that transform realities in a meaningful way. The principle of solidarity economy can be built by individuals and assumes responsibility for the situation at hand, which is characterized by extreme poverty and marginalization.

Throughout many years these problems have been allowed to worsen and now seem impossible to resolve. For example, with respect to agricultural work, it is not possible to immediately abandon the use of agro-chemicals since widespread use of them has been encouraged over a 40-year span. The same can be said about genetically modified seeds and the system of agricultural production in general, which depletes resources and foments the complete destruction of the land, both literally and in a holistic sense.

To recover the land holistically, an alternative, more sustainable agriculture is needed, i.e. agroecology. This implies recovering soil and implementing new systems for seed production and organic fertilizer that allow for the defense of territory and yield an adequate production of diverse foods that guarantee food security and the possibility of bartering products. The overall goal is to respect nature and rediscover the land's potential. Therefore, the relationship between the land and self and one's self with the land is very important. From there, the symbolic element of the universe emerges. The universe is found in culture, history, and the traditions of Indigenous communities. It is a force that determines all of existence.

Solidarity economy is a practice of collective production, exchange, relationships, construction, and work. Organized communities are mindful of new generations, so this economy assumes the participation of children, adults, elders through storytelling, organizing capacity, and their collective vision for the future. From there arises the need to renew forests, conserve water, find solutions to waste, and be vigilant toward industrial chemical contamination.

This vision demands making decisions such as opposing pesticides, genetically modified seeds, agricultural practices that devastate natural resources, and state-sponsored programs that deliver agrochemicals to farmers and target production for international markets. This transformative concept comes from modest practices; it emerged from our strength simultaneously as we became aware that it is possible to generate new alternatives. This didn't just happen in one place, but rather all over the world; this practice of recovery is not constructed only by trying to get out of poverty and marginalization, but also with alternatives to the neoliberal model.

An alternative economy, in a way, reflects the society we want in the future. Given how the neoliberal economy has taken us to war, destruction, competition, and individualism; solidarity economy is an instrument for the construction of new worlds. This economy represents the defense of territory and the search for change to the social relations of production, which are based in the logic of subjugation, racism, and relationships of inequity and abuse.

Solidarity economy is anchored to autonomy, freedom, and all emancipatory processes; it is the construction of resiliance as a strategy of resistance, finding the rhythm of the universe in order to work within the dynamic of totality and not accumulation, dispossession, and destruction. That is, it is about allocating resources in a way that coincides with life, abundance, solidarity, and creating new energies. This is why it does not represent the depletion of resources but rather the permanent renovation of each being, unit, and molecule. Therefore, it is a labor of discovery, understanding, and comprehension, whose objective is to reach a synthesis between every action we take today and our deepest utopias.

Now, to whom is this book directed? To everyone constructing alternatives to capitalism; to fortify the path for those who can see the reality and the potential of what may come to the youth; to new generations; to the rebels, who are willing to transform the relationships of domination and deceit; and to everyone who will have to rebuild and uplift hope after the catastrophe and chaos of the final struggle.

Introduction, Objectives, and Approach

MY INTENTION WAS TO WRITE A MANUSCRIPT THAT WOULD SERVE THE MASSES, which meant it was important to write the book thinking about what the reader would need to construct alternatives and believe in their ability to confront any obstacle with creativity and personal resolve.

I want this to be an invitation to imagine worlds; to face our current situation; to encourage you to take action in a context that seeks to determine and define our actions; to incite you to construct yourselves as transformative subjects of our current reality with an eye towards the future, understanding the seriousness and the strength of actions, as well as the determination behind what is decided and done towards the end of achieving freedom, justice, and the realization of people. In other words, to understand the commitment and energy of others, and that which takes place inside of us, so that we can live fully.

On this journey, we will encounter transformative and powerful energy, light, inspiration and the desire to live. We will strengthen our bodies, open our minds and hearts, our cells will be revitalized, we will open our eyes. We will be creative. We will take ownership over our lives and reality. We will understand other families' histories and other peoples. We will share dreams, learn new things, discover the ability to love, surrender, tenderness, and above all else, we will release our fear to cultivate that which life itself gives in abundance.

The intention is to dislodge lethargy, transform relationships, and to believe again in the creative force within us, revive the experience of transformation to propel processes for social change, new ways of being, thinking, and relating without deceit, submission, or anguish but rather with trust, truth, exchange, respect, and a sense of freedom to live in plentitude. But how do we build a house for all? How do we live in plenitude and how do we ensure the value of enlightenment?

In this way, the purpose of this book coincides with the practice of transforming reality so we can be free in every sense and as part of a society with a global vision. As such, this document is the synthesis of a reflection that emerges from participating in various social, political, economic, cultural, and organizational processes, and can be read in two respects. On the one hand, there is the effort to comprehend the complexity of relationships involving humiliation, discrimination, exploitation and dispossession; and on the other, the construction of alternatives to the neoliberal system that generates deterioration and war.

Likewise, due to the reality in which we live and feel, our work seeks to establish a new order, the construction of a future where the conditions for life, dignity, justice, freedom, and our shared home may be possible. For that to happen, we need to understand our historic responsibility and take on the necessary tasks so that we may transform ourselves while resisting and renouncing the relationships and mechanisms of subjugation. We need to enter alternative dimensions of existence; offer mutual support; walk firmly the path of autonomy, solidarity, social economy, and that which gets us close to profound change—hope. We need to learn to walk the path in obscurity and not falter, listening to the testimonies of those whose work speaks for itself, those who stand firm in their decisions, those who have not abandoned the plow and advance with an eye toward the horizon.

Language and Expression

I HAVE TRIED TO WRITE IN A WAY THAT RESONATES ON A PERSONAL LEVEL SO READERS CAN ENGAGE WITH THIS TEXT IN A CREATIVE AND INSPIRATIONAL WAY, and so they can build their own visions—the kinds of expressions that come from deep down and, at the same time, refer back to the process of theoretical reflection. In this way, it is an ongoing attempt for words, phrases or ways of thinking to be based in reality, social movements, and that which is concrete. My intention is for each chapter to have its own essence and be able to stand on its own; in any case, I have meant for this to be a harmonious body of work, one that could become a tool for understanding political solidarity economy.

Similarly, it tries to shed light on the peasant and Indigenous peoples' historical resistance and the reality of existing alternatives to the global neoliberal model. This is why the invitation to experience this book is itself a tool to discover the potential of this historical moment and transform relationships of exploitation.

This way of being that emerges from collective work; in solidarity with communities and peoples of distinct religions, political parties, and languages; starting with the land and light of each day—that is the future, and it is in the hands of those who want to get involved. It is the power of continuing on this path of ongoing transformation.

In Chiapas, you can see the will of the people surging in outright rebellion. They rebel against the past, in memory of the past, and in memory of utopia and alternative social models. All of this happens in the heart of communities, so close to the past and the future, each being integral to the other.

It is that same land that transforms, takes on a different hue, and accumulates new vitality in order to bear new fruit. It is the greenery and the rain that flourishes on a sunny day in winter, spring, fall, or summer.

They are planting the fields, seeds are sprouting, and from the daily toil—with broad, collective support—the trust that there is life in death is sustained, each being so close to the other.

Within these ongoing contradictions, the real possibility for changing unjust relationships is born along with the existence of men and women who are free to build immense avenues, plazas, markets, and spaces, in order to reinvent themselves.

The reality of poverty and the struggle to escape poverty are real. There are reasons to live and struggle to get out of poverty.

These routes come from afar to guide us to remain loyal to our reason for existence, as fish, as birds, as the ocean, as wind in the spiral of ongoing transformation (Santiago, 2001, p. 107-111).

Chapter One

Walking Toward the Future

1.1 Conceptual Antecedents and the Practice of Solidarity Economy

THE CONCEPTUAL ANTECEDENTS AND THE PRACTICE OF SOLIDARITY ECONOMY respond to the idea of rescuing some reflections from articles, conferences, interviews, and contributions that took place in Canada, the United States, Haiti, Italy, Belgium, the UK, Finland, China, Basque country, Senegal, and Mexico, mostly Chiapas.

After returning from the Third International Encounter for the Globalization of Solidarity in Dakar, Senegal—organized by the Intercontinental Network for Social and Solidarity Economy (RIPESS) in November 2005—Antonio Soriano and Laure de Saint Phalle interviewed me for the French journal *Chimeres* (2006, p. 177-200). After that, *Christus*, a Spanish journal, also published parts of that same interview. Here is that version.

An Interview with Jorge Santiago

Jorge Santiago is a staff member of the organization DESMI with more than 30 years of experience in solidarity economy with Indigenous communities in Chiapas.

What is solidarity economy?

The fundamental element of solidarity economy is the construction of an economic alternative to poverty and marginalization. Capitalism's neoliberal phase produces marginalization as a direct result of a system of wealth accumulation. This is how the proposal for a solidarity economy was born, as a potential alternative model to neoliberalism. This occurred through reflection and analysis of social practice. It is the result of people coming together in groups, collectives, and cooperatives to present common solutions to healthcare, housing, and nutrition.

People of the 'Third World' in Africa, Asia and Latin America, as well as people in Europe, the US and Canada, introduced the concept as far back as the 1940s, when they decided to organize the economy based on mutual collaboration. Beginning in the 1980s to the present, it has become increasingly evident that development without self-determination is impossible and that development without basic sustenance and sustainability is impossible.

What exactly does that mean? It means that you must begin with organized social subjects who are clear about what is required to construct alternatives, departing from the local to the regional, national and international; with the understanding that local issues are tied to the global domination established by groups of organized power, in particular the Group of 8 (G-8), and that relate to the distribution and total control over the world's resources.

Since the 1980s, the poor have become increasingly aware of the economic crisis they live in and contemplate on how the gap between the haves and have-nots has widened, despite all the organized struggles they have waged. This situation has made them think about the possibility to change it: the construction of an alternative model that begins with the recuperation of the experience of self-determination, the ability to exercise rights, and above all, the efficacy in the construction of an alternative model in terms of production, commercialization, services, and consumption.

Sustainability is fundamental to development because it must be rooted in the use of resources that people have generated and constructed for themselves, rather than in the use of all resources available. How is this achieved? Well, you do it through tools such as organic fertilizers, the restoration of soil, defending the land, planning, and taking into account the diversity or all the possibilities when you bring together self-sustaining elements, to leave monoculture behind and create the conditions needed to grow polyvalent crops.

All of this brings forth an understanding that reality has a pluralistic sentiment. This capacity of creating resources also implies a cultural element, and this culture emerges from the knowledge that exists in the world and a history of resistance. The knowledge about how to conserve organic seeds, how to conserve genetic knowledge when it comes to animals, plants, and health. The discovery of different codices, to the extent that people live in different ways, in terms of social organization, elements that are found in the organizational and the political. When all of this is understood in its minutia, one understands that at the base of all resistance, there is a different model and that when you strengthen that base, the possibility of another world can be constructed.

It is a world that also positions itself as another possible economy. When it reaches this level, conversations about the value of cooperation, solidarity, and exchange begin, which go beyond money and goods. It is then possible to consider the notion of the "gift" that comes from Marcel Mauss, that societies are based on the gift, through exchange, through the search for ethics, through human behavior, centering people, rather than goods or money (1925).

When that which came before is revived, solidarity economy begins to germinate. Naming it thusly, it is elevated above the models that came before, which were merely social constructions of cooperation, mutualities that continue to exist and that are still the foundation of many things, but that did not have the consciousness of the construction of another model, they were only aware of their participation in it.

A solidarity economy will require a different model of society. When this need is discovered, one must consider how to move it forward. You can't assume it will ignite spontaneously, but rather, that it will provide the initial spark to fuel a movement. Examples include the Exchange Network to Strengthen Solidarity Economy Processes, which met in Lima, Peru in 1997, then in Quebec in 2001, and Senegal in 2005, followed by a fourth meeting in Belgium that was announced in the Dakar, Senegal statement in 2007 as part of a network called North-South, which constituted an initial gathering around two possibilities--the Global North and Global South which came together as one system to promote this type of economy. Today, the gatherings are particularly concerned with continuing the refinement of this concept. In other words, solidarity economy is a work in progress and will continue to be constructed. Some discover it in practice, without knowing they are already creating a solidarity economy.

Others recognize that if there are no political objectives to transform reality, if there is no social counterweight, if we do not strengthen people's ability to negotiate with the global structures of market control, such as the International Monetary Fund (IMF), the World Bank, or the World Trade Organization, we could say that despite creating a solidarity economy, it may end up still being a marginalized economy.

Therefore, strengthening people's ability to negotiate with said global structures is important so they can answer to the interests of our people: such as defending local agriculture, addressing rising global inequality, and the overproduction of some countries which stamps out local farmers. If they are unable to stop rich countries from continuing to increase production through the advantage of subsidies and if they are unable to create new international laws, the solidarity economy may end up being a marginal economy.

Hence, the solution to making sure it is not marginalized is in [establishing] networks, because the foundation of solidarity economy is based on networks.

How do you structure a network? How does an organization that wants to join the network become a part of it?

The concept of the network is new. It is constructed with different interrelationships. It is like a fishing net made up of crisscrossing lines that reinforce one another. The strength of the fish net is two-fold: the intersecting lines support one another, and together, they support the net as a whole. There is no central point, but rather the weight is distributed throughout the entire net, which is what makes action possible. In other words, what you have in the net is the possibility, of a global construction. The negative and the positive, the specific and the global, are also important elements.

Network construction implies, fundamentally, participation within the whole. It is not the search for a singular direction, but rather the search for a collective strength. In other words, to participate in the network means to depart from self-organization and a singular identity. Although the network incorporates the idea of a singular net, as used by fishermen, it also incorporates the idea of a network in terms of a plurality of relationships, made up of different identities and intensities.

Establishing this concept demonstrates the possibility of growth. How does one grow? You grow from the need to get stronger. It is not about the exclusion of others, but rather about the integration of others; those who have the intention of creating networks, structures, world organizations, alternative processes, and those with the intention of building a people's international solidarity.

Take, for example, what is happening in Chiapas. The emergence of the EZLN creates conditions for bonds of solidarity to exist in the world. Those who create networks are those most interested in solidarity existing because they are the same organizations who have been struggling for many years to address hunger, food, micro-loans, migration, health, HIV/AIDS, human rights, women's rights, children's rights, disability rights, refugees, domestic violence, those displaced off their lands, or by earthquakes and tsunamis, and struggles for freedom, climate, among others. Those developing networks are creating impactful conditions so these things no longer happen.

These organizations discovered that the way to move forward is to create these networks. Basically, in this solidarity economy, there is a need to work to unite all of our experiences. The possibilities and priorities are global now are global and can be thought of as the "globalization of hope." This commitment has provoked a strategy to invest resources in global movements that propose alternatives. The global social forums held in Brazil, India, Pakistan, Africa, and Venezuela are one such example. This possibility has all the momentum to create conditions of interrelatedness so that different processes can begin to integrate with one other and so that participation can be consolidated from the local to the regional to the national and finally, the international. Intercontinental networks have been developing the last eight years in Lima, Quebec, and Senegal. The effort there is to highlight how important it is to build intercontinental networks.

These encounters come from and serve civil society as a practical effort to bring about public policies or dialogues with governments so that they may act in accordance with social interests. In a way, governments are convened so that they may be supportive but governments are not convened to present their proposals. In these dialogues, civil society is not asking governments for their contribution in terms of development, social assistance, but rather, governments are asked to exert their ability to defend national interests in the face of transnational interests.

Another important point is that [global] integration emerges from local practices and work done at the local level. The objective is to strengthen peoples' struggle, local structures, each entity's organizing forms—so that the organizing emerges from us and responds to our needs—this is what is being invented. It is to create the process of construction, where we are the subjects, because otherwise, we may end up creating yet another superstructure that reflects the interests of organisms and institutions that say they operate at a global level, yet essentially represent nothing.

The challenge is that participation in these events or in these mobilizations comes from those who have roots and experience working as a whole made up of different roots, to avoid the homogenization of the world in terms of globalization. The ultimate goal lies in the ability of each community and each organization to have a dignified life, sustainability, and the ability to exist in the world, to give and provide resources, and participate in the construction of their own lives, rather than passively receive help and support as victims, i.e. people who need the 'First World' to save them from their troubles. They should be part of the world because they have their own skills, which many times have been obscured because they have been rejected or because the wisdom of the people has not been considered a fundamental part of humanity's patrimony.

Do these networks exist in Europe?

Since the fall of the Berlin Wall in 1989, there has been concern in Europe about the integration of the East, as well as the expansion of the East, its history and identity. There is a gap in terms of technology, opportunity, capacity, and employment, as well as in the damage wrought upon youth and farmer participation by the development of socialism in the East. In reality, Europe has challenges that are very important to solve: unemployment, homelessness, health and aging populations. These can be resolved through a solidarity economy.

There are some European solidarity entities that are now looking at their own countries and considering the transformation of local relationships to create elements of this global construction. Participants come to the intercontinental gatherings to showcase this innovation. The globalization of the capitalist model which is now in its neoliberal stage also creates negative consequences in the countries considered to be first world nations. It is not only nations of the Global South that are affected, but Europe too. It is the same model that generates waste and exclusion, and does not have the capacity to solve the problems it creates. This is why the realization of the need for change continues to grow in the south just as much as it does in the north.

Participants in this process are young people from the Global North who feel they have no alternatives within the system. They are young people who are able to navigate the system via technology. They understand it and speak with one another. They are aware of what is happening in other parts of the world and they engage in a shared journey with far away peoples. They are trying to escape the European world. They are saying that life exists beyond this model, as well as beyond their own space. Why live in the system and fight to have a place when there are infinite possibilities outside of the system? This is a rupture.

In the beginning you said that the networks created are the ones that support existing organizations: European or Canadian or American. Is there fear that these organizations will influence these networks with European or Western ideas?

It's the problem of control, those who are more interested in the construction of these networks are the ones who also need to create alternatives. They are going to disseminate a model of participation that is a bit like creating the model for development. They will contribute to the peoples' development but they are not going to conduct social welfare. They will call for the people to organize, to get involved, and they will provide them with a share of resources through loans […] they'll no longer provide social welfare.

Therefore, it will be like creating a third model at the level of networks, no longer at the level of people, individuals, or nations. The point of departure is that the process of constructing networks—at the local or national level—had already come into existence. This is to say that there already existed an experience of the construction of relationships among Indigenous peoples.

There is another element within the struggles for land, such as the Landless Workers' Movement in Brazil. In Africa, there is a movement that works to recover land, soils and biotechnology. The EZLN movement is a movement in the process of constructing Indigenous peoples' rights.

All this is happening during a moment in which, on the one hand, strength is emerging from the people, and on the other, you have these organizational proposals. We have to create the possibility for dialogue and not focus on the fight for power. What rationale will remain or how will all this ultimately be systematized?

They asked us what we have to gain, to win, those of us from the Global South, from participating in this networking process that comes from organizations in the North, so I flipped the question. What does the North gain if we participate? In other words, it is mutual. Because that is where the strategy lies in addition to the possibility of the Global South considering our proposals in expansive terms of exchange and shared responsibility, refusing the idea that the Global North finances the actions of the Global South. Rather, it is a construction of shared resources. And when constructing networks, they must be completely sustainable—not sustainable in the Global North with some benefit in the Global South. This has to do with the concept of development.

Countries in the Global South can participate in an economy with fair trade products where raw materials are valued, and the hours of labor dedicated to the manufacturing of products throughout the world are valued. So that people can value what it means to have coffee, tea, flour or sugar, assuming that other terms of value also exist. There are enough resources for us to build a global alternative together. Dependency is not needed, but rather recognition; and this has yet to be established. Yes, there is racism but there is also submission. People discriminate because they do not value their own history. And there are models of competition because people also do not accept their own limitations and wealth. Therefore, when the people recognize that their own identity has value and that they are not competing with others, then we can say we are mutual collaborators working towards the common good.

In the Philippines, they said: "We need resources, what will we do?" A million people gave small amounts of money which created immense capital that became *their* capital. With this exercise […] they no longer needed credit from the World Bank, they had their own credit.

Experiences with creating our own monetary systems are also expanding because they are based on trust. You say, " I believe in the Euro because I believe that I can eat with the 100 Euros I have." And they give me 100 Euros and I believe it has value. I trust that I will be able to pay for my home or whatever. We establish trust via a different mechanism, just like during the meeting we arranged. New currencies are established outside of the official currency and acquire value as people believe in them. We hope that each system of construction of alternative currencies creates a network of sustainability and an institution that protects them. Alternative currencies are moving towards the possibility of combining with different experiences. There are very important experiences in China, where alternatives are being proposed, including a new currency. This will strengthen movements because moving away from the dominance of the Euro, the US dollar, the yen, or to simply escape economic control and build one's own system, is strength.

The elements of these alternatives have existed since the 1950s. It is not new but rather the beginning of a process that will take a long time. It will take many years to consolidate a system that is different from the one in which we are living. We cannot avoid this destiny.

What will you do when capitalism realizes that solidarity economy will be very dangerous? Don't you think that this will bring about a very difficult struggle? How are you preparing for that?

Since the beginning we have known there will be a confrontation: to overcome the fear of not having a boss. The very moment you do that, in the moment you overcome a world with bosses, is when you are able to defend yourself from the boss.

In your view, does fair trade belong to a solidarity economy, or are they unrelated?

The idea of fair trade has emerged as a proposal of exchange, from the valuation of the processes of production, with quality certifications, a just distribution of benefits, and the possibility of uniting producers with consumers.

[However], fair trade certification costs a lot of money. So, the institutions that have positioned themselves as providers of certifications are operating in a way that garners them benefits and speculative profits. Also, given they are based in countries of the Global North, they compete in the market.

They are part of the system in a particular way.

They are able to establish channels of commerce but within the system. Take coffee, honey, and textiles as an example. Fair trade of these goods is an example of unilateral development. It has the possibility of creating conditions for fair exchange, but it has to strengthen the local environment. As it turns out, fair trade has yielded better prices with the products exported by small producers, but they still have to organize themselves to grow their own food. There also may be several organizations in the same region that sell fair trade coffee, which gives rise to competition among these producers in order to see who can sell more. Given this, some people turn towards fair trade over a solidarity economy. In other words, despite its organizing process, fair trade lacks an integral vision of sustainability in the long-term, and the ability to create systems that don't repeat structures of wealth accumulation.

Within this process, some people also consider that fair trade cannot strengthen territorial rights and identities, and above all that the entrapment of commercialization will always generate, in one way or another, exploitation within the same system.

The coffee producers in Chiapas, for example, are selling fair trade coffee at the market price under the United States' North American Free Trade Agreement (NAFTA). In the course of my work in Chiapas, with thirty-five years of social practice and research within community organizations, when we discuss an alternative to marginalization and exploitation, we put forth political solidarity economy.

When we work in a community and say "let's build a solidarity economy," we build an integrated vision in such a manner that it can be said that economy is communication, fair relationships, rights, housing, and health. Health is the economy, and it is not possible to sustain a health system that is commercialized. Therefore, if you build conditions for wellness, you build a solidarity economy.

Chiapas, Mexico

In present-day Chiapas, Mexico, the troubling dynamic which prioritizes state interests in strategic resources can be traced back to the 1960s. The colonization of the Lacandona

Jungle in Chiapas initiated a movement towards liberation. The aforementioned situation was the first experience toward an understanding of liberation of the oppressed—a fundamental historical precedent that enabled the emergence of several important social movements.

The enduring concentration of economic and political power in the hands of a few has long coincided with the logic of the capitalist, now neoliberal, system. In contrast, community involvement in the ongoing search for liberation, organizing processes, defense of territory, and community resistance is integrated into a strategy for autonomy and self-determination, based on a vision of building a new refuge where we may all co-exist.

On the other hand, we also find the church-led liberation movement, which first serves the people with their organizing processes. We also have the Autochthonous Church, which incites hope illuminated by the spirit. There, you also encounter a practical method to evangelize which takes into account the social reality and cultural elements, and practices a methodology to achieve the emergence of community-led dialogue with which evangelists become a receiver for the community. This methodology allows for the discovery and ability to articulate one's own dialogue. Theological reflection, based on events and the understand to discover Indigenous cosmology, is a local and regional reality.

There were also evangelical churches and ecumenical efforts that assumed a political commitment to transform relationships of domination and build strategies to create a permanent sense of hope. This commitment drove the pastoral agents of the Diocese of San Cristóbal de Las Casas, following Don Samuel's example, to mediate conflicts. This is how the organization of pastoral work began, taking into account ethnic diversity and the participation of women, men, youth, and elders as responsible for their own destiny, accompanied by rhythm, the silence of the mountains, songs, dance, prayer, fasting, and *fiestas* to share and walk the path together.

In such a manner, collective action is a way to defend territory, produce food, work with different collectives through mutual agreements and decisions, while learning to build relationships and organizations with the intention of reinforcing plans to escape the reality of domination and erasure. Accordingly, not everything that happens now can be considered a path to liberty; nevertheless, in the multitude of efforts and work that is being carried out, the seeds of freedom appear.

The Challenges

Growing within the continuity of history is a fundamental challenge. This is to say, it is an awakening that has taken many years, made possible by the participation and massive power present in communities and in the consciousness of the people and in the hearts of women and men who continue the work of struggling to transform unjust relationships, with the ultimate goal of sustaining an alternative vision of a world where the structures of domination; mechanisms of manipulation and control by the state, entrepreneurs, and those privileged by the capitalist system, which in essence is a structure based on generating wealth through dispossession, extortion, repression, and death; have been replaced.

Therefore, it is important to recognize and deeply understand the resulting social movements as part of the process to transform the current power structure. These concrete struggles are rooted in the daily life of communities, the same struggles where hope is found, which is why the challenge lies in recognizing what these struggles teach us through vital, life-affirming experiences that represent long-term radical options as a product of reflection, praxis, and the convictions of individuals and communities with a high degree of knowledge and wisdom.

This path is an alternative to submission, a path that will not take us back to the place we are leaving behind. Hence, when we build a refuge for all and defend territory, we are simultaneously seeking reconciliation and dialogue. When we see each other and listen to one another, we commit to working together as a collective, and we invent the mechanisms to resist everyday, maintaining unity, integrating our past into the future, and living in the present with abundance in order to root ourselves to our land and community with our parents and siblings.

This is what keeps us alive insomuch as we want to establish a place of mutual respect and participation, with honesty and the ability to transform submissive relationships, and build a community for the well-being of all. As such, peace, justice, and dignity will be the result of this massive effort.

1.2 Political Solidarity Economy

Solidarity economy is an alternative structure that allows us to unify histories of resistance with various searches for alternatives. It is a practice of constructing alternatives that derive from the practice of autonomy, justice, solidarity and creativity among those who suffer from the deterioration of the quality of life under the neoliberal system.

A Process of Reflection Derived From Practice

There is a fundamental challenge in all movements that emerge from the people that concerns the search for ways to escape poverty and the structural marginalization of the capitalist neoliberal system. This challenge is made more evident with the system in crisis, because under dire circumstances, neoliberalism's strategy becomes clearer and more aggressive.

The way in which capitalism operates, especially in Chiapas and Mexico as a whole, is crude and without consideration, given how it consists of dispossession, profit, the accumulation and concentration of power, political control over resources and markets, the negation of history, impunity, the ideology of domination, the negation of rights, abuse, death, war, militarization, processes of social decay, the deterioration of the social fabric, and human and drug trafficking. As such, individualism, competition, and the cult of the strongest have the capacity to make life meaningless.

In this way, political solidarity economy is the search to replace a model of production rooted in unjust relationships, with a model based on the principles of exchange, respect for nature, and commitment to others, and whose objective is to produce, create, construct and transform.

In this way, a political solidarity economy is built through practice. This entails collective action by people who consciously participate in a process that stems from the analysis of poverty, marginalization, and the violation of universal human rights. It is therefore a strategic action that addresses every critical element of capitalism's system and structure: individual interests, depletion of resources, accumulation of power, profit, and destruction.

Political solidarity economy relates to the process of production and exchange, and consequently, the market and more expansive relationships in society. It concerns the construction of knowledge and technologies that take into account an understanding of the whole, and at the same time, make possible a safe and healthy future for new generations to establish a respectful relationship with nature and the sources of life, while compelling us to take transformative action and cease the indiscriminate use of resources.

Political solidarity economy is the construction of alternatives from the perspective of an alternative model of society. It involves identifying and taking concrete steps in the opposite direction of profit and domination. It is an action rooted in the histories of the people and their deep yearnings; the history of resistance and liberation; the interaction between the forces of nature and the potential of each being. In sum, it is the encounter with the seeds of liberation.

The true transformative act is borne from the consciousness and determination to no longer perpetuate and uphold the mechanisms of power that impose and deny the rights of others. Therefore, political solidarity economy represents the place where dreams are born, where experimentation and the journey to freedom are possible.

Solidarity economy is the construction of hope that comes with collective participation, self-reliance, solidarity, and the realization of the power of dialogue.

It is knowledge derived from experience; it is the vitality of women who wake up at dawn to bless the day with renewed effort to maintain life in each action and offering.

The decision to build political solidarity economy implies collective learning and is based on a series of decisions such as: to become active, to become subjects of the future, to be aware of reality, to overcome conditions of poverty and political and social marginalization in which we find ourselves due to the structural exclusion from the capitalist system, and to convince ourselves that the situation will change if we actively engage in the transformation of reality in an organized manner.

This process has gained strength in Chiapas through the autonomy established by the EZLN.[1] The practice of resistance and the Zapatistas' autonomy have shown, with great clarity, what an alternative solidarity economy looks like, along with its emphasis on defending strategic resources, such as land, and on collective ownership of modes of production.

In this way, political solidarity economy, as a system, is part of an expansive alternative model, one that is all-encompassing and complex. It is a model built with the autonomy and resistance of Indigenous peoples, through which the creation of another economy becomes the way towards transforming conditions of injustice and oppression.

The fundamental element of political solidarity economy symbolizes the construction of an economic alternative in response to the reality of poverty and marginalization that involves the people taking action and organizing themselves, which is why it is a long and arduous path.

Within the same concept of political solidarity economy, there is breadth; recognition of diverse processes and actors; various dimensions; and the need to continue consolidating solidarity networks; regional, national, and international relationships; as well as to be present in the plan to recover our collective resources, through which conditions for a dignified life can be established.

There is a strong link between political solidarity economy and community struggles to establish autonomy. Within these struggles—whether economic, political, social, or cultural—there is the fight for the universal rights of freedom, democracy, independence, the recognition of the rights of women and Indigenous communities, the right to land, self-determination, and freedom of choice.

Sources

There are many resources and writings about solidarity economy. I consider the Intercontinental Network of Social Solidarity Economy (RIPESS, in its Spanish acronym) of greater relevance given its significance in Canada and Latin America for its role in building this information network and

---

1   The EZLN was founded on November 17th, 1983 in the Lacandona Jungle, Chiapas.

promoting social and solidarity economy. Likewise, there are various sources of information in which different research and analytical works have been published, meaning that each region of the world has a history in the construction process. In Chiapas, for example, we learned to build with the autonomy and resistance of Indigenous communities. Hence, it is important to understand solidarity economy within the context of land defense, strategic resources, and the rights of Indigenous communities in relation to the San Andrés Accords concerning Indigenous Rights and Culture (1996).

The San Andrés Accords on Indigenous Rights and Culture are found in a document signed by the Mexican government and the Zapatista Army for National Liberation on February 16, 1996, thereby committing to modify the Mexican constitution to recognize the rights of Indigenous people. However, the Congress and Senate did not ratify these agreements.

From 2001 to 2008, the Institution for the Social Economic Development of Indigenous Mexicans (DESMI, in its Spanish acronym) held eight annual solidarity economy meetings in San Cristóbal de las Casas, Chiapas, with the participation of representatives from different autonomous communities in Chiapas, and from the rest of Mexico, along with communities from Guatemala, El Salvador, Nicaragua, Haiti, Italy, France, Spain, the United States, Canada, the United Kingdom, Belgium, Holland, Switzerland, Norway and Japan.

DESMI has been in Chiapas since 1969, taking its first steps alongside Indigenous and farming communities. As one of its main lines of work, this organization has taken on economic action by supporting community initiatives with administrative counseling, programming, analysis, agroecological technologies, and the discovery of strategic objectives for which it is necessary to organize and work. One of these is the construction of a solidarity economy, which has received the support of international development cooperation agencies.

With regard to the experience of Zapatista communities, there are also various studies, sources of information, and reflections on the construction of alternatives in a context of counterinsurgency and how the practice of alternatives becomes the building of Indigenous people's autonomy (see González and Garcia, 2008).

The book *Luchas "Muy Otras": Zapatismo y autonomía en las comunidades Indígenas de Chiapas* (Baronnet, Mora and Stahler-Sholk, 2011) is the result of an investigation committed to autonomous communities in the process of constructing alternatives, which are rooted in the dedication of the many who envision the future as their own and accept their historical responsibility for participating in it.

Lessons from the Struggle

In 2004, I finished my 30-year tenure as DESMI coordinator. Upon stepping down, I crafted a document entitled *Lessons from Struggling Together*, from which I extracted some paragraphs to help us understand the political solidarity economy in the process of construction:

They want war

We want peace with justice and dignity

They want to make us disappear

And we want everyone to live

They want to deny us

And we want to exist

They want to dominate us

And we want equality

They want to turn us into goods

And we want respect

They plot to destroy us

And we build

They forget

And we remember

They walk towards the past

And we see the horizon of a new era

For all

1.3 DESMI's Task: Looking Toward the Future

THE NEW STAGE IS PEACEFUL, A NEW AWAKENING. A series of historical processes have taken place in which we can clearly see that those who are deciding on their way of life are those who have assumed the challenge imposed by history to build their future with their own hands, through their own effort.

These individuals are capable of deciding since they also demonstrate the capacity to act in an organized manner with precise goals. This new stage requires a high degree of efficacy, which is why we must build a new world with dedication, care, precision, viability, and legitimacy.

It is a stage in which there can be no fear, as the pathway to liberation is laden with freedom and dignity. This implies the possibility of something besides the imposed model. The possibility to build something new is a given—this is why we call it a new stage.

We no longer have to fight to open the door to the future. We now have the steps, so we will walk in the indicated direction, which implies resistance on the autonomous path of autonomy. Therefore, it is a transformation of the relations of power and submission; it is the construction of alternatives like a beautiful dream that allows us to decolonize our thinking and form new images and realities.

This is a critical stage, as it establishes the conflict between past and future. It is a conflict between those who fight to maintain existing structures of domination and those who struggle to establish equality, respect, the capacity to listen, and the capacity to work together towards a common horizon.

This new stage requires learning and training to bring forth the new; it requires us to fill ourselves with light to live enlightened. In this way, we need to transform ourselves, change perspective, decide either unilaterally or together, in accordance with our vision, a common vision, or solely from our thoughts and seek dialogue with each and every person.

What are the tasks of this stage?

→ Strengthen the proposal for sovereignty of the people over their territory, the right to enjoy their resources, healthy food production, and just relationships in an equitable society.

→ Continue to build the path to achieve respect for the rights and dignity of women, thereby reaching equality between women and men.

→ Learn everything needed to live in peace, building a better future for the well-being of each and everyone.

→ Prepare ourselves with the rigor required to confront the problems of the world through solidarity and the sharing of what we have.

→ Present ourselves according to what we say or think, to start from a commitment to ourselves.

→ Understand the new circumstances of reality, which are meaningless if not linked to everyone's destiny since when we act in a specific context, we do so from the perspective of broader transformations. Therefore, it is important to understand the context in which we move and act accordingly.

→ Participate in a common construction, which requires breaking away from isolation, overcoming the fear of approaching what arises or appears in spaces that we do not know.

What emerges?

→ The certainty that there is a new world, which is built from below and recognizes the knowledge accumulated in the experience of praxis.

→ Knowledge that is made up of everyone's contributions, which is open to innovation and surprises; comes in many shades, dimensions, concerns, doubts; is rational; is established in opposition; is not fixed; and is in permanent transformation.

→ Knowledge that always establishes possibilities, does not close itself off, takes the shape of a spiral, and must grow.

→ Knowledge that grows in multiple dimensions: up, down, from side to side, from the deepest depths to the highest peaks, and has the possibilities of a totality, made up of varieties.

→ The need to overcome the global crisis created by established powers with an alternative power; born with conviction, the satisfaction to establish wellness for all, and sharing everything with everyone.

→ The dimension of the global as it pertains to the shared history of living beings, since we are beings with a shared destiny with nature and with all people.

This identity is the guarantee that if we search for the essence or heart of others, we will find the possibility to be brothers and sisters, together, as *compañeras* and *compañeros*.[2] In this way, the conviction that no one is superior to anyone else emerges, reminding us that we owe each other respect, rights, and the obligation to take care of each other and protect our resources for life. We will not survive and be able to work towards the future of new generations if we do not take care of the water, the land, the forests, the plants, the animals, and the seeds.

Thus, an understanding emerges of the differences that exist between men and women, generations of children, young people, elders, languages and customs, and the different

---

2   *Compañer(a/o)* does not have a direct translation but is similar to the idea of comrade. It means one who accompanies another along a path, or a walk, or a journey.

ways of thinking which respond to the fundamental challenge of moving towards coexistence and dialogue. This implies that the alternatives to the situation of domination must establish the possibility to face our differences.

In sum, society's movement, in which people participate from different origins chart the same course, is emerging. To recognize difference as a point of departure and walk together is the task.

What Must Continue

We must continue the practice of organized work, the search for concrete results while overcoming the limitations of technology and communication. We must continue the construction of resources using the ones we already have and grow in different dimensions. We must learn from experience—from the process, from being part of the movement—to share our history. We must maintain the bonds that make us stronger and more capable to weather the storm, as with the call to action, since there is still a need for many people, communities, and regions to join in the struggle for shared liberation. Therefore, we must move forward with the joy of being alive because while our presence exists, we can give life.

The Method To Continue The Struggle

When we think we have a future objective, we believe that we will reach our goal when we arrive. The method of continuing to walk implies that to the extent that we are working to achieve the objective, what we are looking for is already present in some way, given that in practice our future is tied to our present. Therefore, we do not seek a potentially new world for the 'after,' but rather, a world that we create in the present because we decided to walk on that path.

An action rooted in the future is an action that makes us live what we strive to find. This corresponds to putting into practice the elements that constitute an alternative such as solidarity, sharing, coming together, listening to one other, making decisions together, contributing, respecting, as well breaking ties, conditioning, fear, authoritarianism and our neglect of others. When we do this type of collective work, we can say that we are making that new world possible. Therefore, the method of continuing to walk is the only one that will bring us closer to what we are looking for.

1.4 The Experience of Feeling, Thinking, and Taking Action

WHAT I WRITE SEEKS TO MODIFY AN OPPRESSIVE AND SUBMISSIVE SYSTEM. The first step in this search relates to a geographic approach that has do to with an understanding of the riches that exist in distinct parts of Chiapas, such as the composition of the soil, the climate, the vegetation, the waterways, the mountains, the lakes, the incredible biodiversity, the flora, the fauna, and the presence of thousand-year old cultures. This action is difficult to fully understand, given that new riches are continuously discovered underground, such as mines, petroleum, etc.—in addition to richness with regard to the notion of life within the culture of communities. Together with the geographic aspect, we find a geopolitic that appears along the border between Chiapas and Central America, and the strategic interests with respect to migration, communications, and the regional control that the United States establishes over our lands, the Caribbean, and South America.

The second act relates to history, the process of colonization, the historic resistance of the people, the depletion of resources, the groups in power, the recent history of plantations, cattle farms, grain products, sugar cane, the new plantations of African palm trees and the proposals for biodiesel production. This strategy corresponds to a group of organizing processes, which arose in 1994 through the EZLN in response to the enacting of the North American Free Trade Act between Canada, the United States, and Mexico. Hence, there is a long history concerning the meaning of territory and the need to defend it. The third act relates to understanding life under a system of relationships of capitalistic exploitation, which we know as the neoliberal capitalist system and which serves as a predatory system with no end in sight, with an emphasis on the accumulation of strategic resources based on the imposed logic of power through a false exercise in democracy, supported by a military occupation strategy endemic to the system of global accumulation perpetrated by international power structures. In this last act, the need to create alternatives to the neoliberal capitalist system is clear as day. As such, political solidarity economy looks to build autonomy and community self-determination, in the sense of a society based on just relations with respect for life and nature. In this way, the above-mentioned is the definition of political solidarity economy.

The process of feeling, thinking, and acting happens within a timeframe that gets longer and longer. I began this journey in Chiapas when I was 26 years old (1969), as part of an ongoing relationship with Indigenous communities, focusing on discrimination, exploitation, humilliation, muted pain, hidden resistance, the silence of the mountains, the hidden say, the "I don't know," and with the feeling of waking up and taking on the sociopolitcal challenges to raise consciousness and assert the necessary presence of others.

It was very important to learn together; to be involved in the life of communities; to learn the rhythm and live in sync with history, the universal time; to learn to interpret the blending of multiple factors such as common space, the territory, the planet, and the universe. I participated in everything and I learned to put that everything into the transformative passion of my body, my feelings, my training, my family, in the same sense as goods and security.

Chapter Two

Geography:
A Fundamental Vision
for the Economy

CHIAPAS IS A STATE IN SOUTHEAST MEXICO, BORDERING GUATEMALA. This land belongs to the Mayan region and stretches across 74,867,127 square kilometers. Based on the 2005 census, the population is roughly 4,293,459 inhabitants. It is a strategically important state for Mexico's development due to the presence of various modes of energy production, such as oil and electricity, forests and jungles, biodiversity, farming and cattle herding.

In this region there are important ethnic groups, such as the Tzeltal, Tzotil, Ch'ol, Zoque, Tojolabal, Mam, Motozintleco, Kaqchikel, Lacandon, Acaltec, and Chuj peoples, who embody a consciousness of resistance and cultural richness.

The history of Chiapas can be understood when you take into account the ongoing rebellions of Indigenous peoples and their resistance to domination, given the theft, labor exploitation, and indignities they have experienced. The exploitation of strategic resources can be considered the principal objective of transnational corporations and military occupation. Despite the fact that the use of resources is fundamental for Chiapas's development, the exploitation of resources by transnational companies obtains greater importance with regard to regional interests and development plans such as the plan for the Tehuantepec Isthmus, the hydroelectric plants along the Usumacinta River, among other projects throughout various regions. It is also important to consider the biodiversity that is found in the Landadona Jungle.

Chiapas, which is located along the border with Central America, and situated between the Atlantic and Pacific oceans, is connected to important river networks and maritime routes that influence weather patterns, precipitation, and the composition of the soil and mountainous terrain. This, in turn, embeds Chiapas in the strategy of resource appropriation by global interests in mining, energy resources, and biodiversity.

At the same time, it is important to consider what Mexico's southern border means to the imperial interests of the United States and Canada, as well as the security mechanisms implemented to safeguard their interests.

Given this, the potential and the pressure of social action are of utmost importance, given that every process of transformation is built on these conditions, their limits and also their possibilities. The defense of territory is an action that is necessary to build an alternative to the system of displacement adherent to the neoliberal strategy; nonetheless, it is not possible to forget that it faces the global interests on which the accumulation of capital depends.

Therefore, it is important to recognize the history of the peoples' resistance, the historic components of their rebellions, and the wisdom of ancestral cultures, which have maintained structures, systems, and strength, while building alternatives over the course of centuries. The recognition of this historical force makes it possible to understand why the strength of the people can be trusted, as they express this type of vitality as they walk.

Within this vast and diverse territory, there are Indigenous, Black, and mestizo populations, as well as an abundance of flora, fauna, minerals, rivers, and mountains. There are also cities where services, power, government are concentrated, as well as various interests in the context of regional, national, and international relationships.

In this way, a road is no more than the neverending flow of all these economic, political, social, cultural signifiers; rebellion; destructive strategies; control mechanisms; and alternatives to the model of subjugation and domination—ultimately, to defend and hopefully achieve the reconstruction of a new sky and a new Earth with justice and dignity for all.

Now, how important is this space where the seeds of freedom grow? The border with Central America is of the utmost importance because of migration and the control of drug trafficking. Historically, it functions as a center of confluence between cultures and commerce. At the same time, there is a cultural identity and a common problem in the destiny of communities. For many years, trade relationships were established based on the sale of wood, rubber, coffee, and energy. There is concern for the conservation of these resources since they can be exploited to enhance industry and regional tourism. This consideration alone is enough to explain the origin of today's conflict with the EZLN.

Almost one million Indigenous people have territorial control over their lands, which allows them to produce using different technologies and adjust to a variety of terrains and climates.

They maintain systems of social and political organization with a sense of community and society; building alternatives in the face of the transnational process; and participating in a broad global phenomenon of communication and use of goods and services as a permanent and growing exchange.

In the past 40 years, there have been massive changes in the region as a result of ground communication, the presence of development plans and the creation of a political agenda to transform the country. Indigenous peoples have driven these changes. They undergo the neverending revision of their actions in these dynamics; it is a movement through which we can observe and experience what these expansive relationships mean at the global level. The capacity for change resides in the identity of the people. Given this, there are people that form within a great diversity and within a broad, intercultural context composed of different economic and political interests.

We support a process of change and mobilization that is enacted by many actors. Farming communities, for example, are changing, and with it everything that they encompass. In this manner, there is an urban population of rural origin with other needs; there are commercial groups that have nothing to do with farming communities as that entails a lack of industrial development, but there is participation in tourism and the service industry. There are then competing conceptions of society and religion; even within different churches, there are varying interpretations of their work. Similarly, the media allows you to keep up with national issues and there appears to be a change in values and political behavior in how these issues are being managed.

Thanks to these mobilizations, we arrive at the notions of self-determination and right to autonomy, as part of an exercise of cultural resistance, as well as an appropriation of people's right to exist—that is, as a cry against erasure and oblivion. This is a requirement to create a proposal as an ethnic group within a multi-ethnic and multicultural nation, taking a stand against marginalization and dependency as a challenge to overcome and building our own alternatives—not within the scheme of continuity under the imposed and colonial model of society, but rather, with one based on elements of cultural identity and universal participation. On the other hand, there is also a conflicting and confrontational situation. The control mechanisms unleashed after the emergence of the EZLN in 1994 by the three levels of government—with a clear logic of counterinsurgency and the complexity of interests over strategic resources over the last few years—have resulted in a space of division and confrontation. At the same time, peoples' resistance remains, along with a series of emerging alternatives that respond to domination and dispossession.

Afrodescendants

The study of Afrodescendants in Chiapas is important to understand the culture and potential of the state, since they have contributed to the economy and makeup of Chiapas society. In rural environments, particularly in Indigenous communities, Afro-mestizos integrated into the culture, contributing structure, vision and appreciation of life, which is manifested in carnivals, dances, and other festivities.

These facts are of utmost importance, considering that the alternatives that have emerged carry a historical force of resistance which is found particularly in Africa, Brazil, Colombia, Cuba, and Mexico.

The Cities

Increasingly complex interests are concentrated in cities, and relate to what is happening in the world. In each region of the state, there is a city with its own problems. In the last 50 years, the urban population grew, which gave rise to a great diversity of religions, political stances, economic situations, as well as a constant influx of farmers, Indigenous peoples, mestizos, and people from other countries.

Systems of communication, institutions, commercial areas, and financial centers were established in cities as job opportunities became more diverse. Peasants and Indigenous people participated in the economy, which created a transformation in relationships.

Thus, a new social subject emerges, rooted in the past, continuously returning to their rural place of origin where they maintain relationships with a new world that is technologically different and establish economic ties with capitalist companies and with national and international tourism, as permanent migrants who are forcibly drawn to different spaces. This movement carries new realities that modify their way of life and conception of work, becoming yet another commodity and distancing themselves from creative work as producers of goods.

Chapter Three
A Historical Context Of Chiapas

AT THE END OF THE 20TH CENTURY, IT CANNOT BE DENIED THAT THE REBELS IN CHIAPAS BECAME A CATALYST FOR BADLY NEEDED CHANGES THROUGHOUT THE COUNTRY. This, in a way, was expressed in the historic defeat of the PRI after 71 years of domination. Having confronted a worn out system, the rebels secured their presence along with a salient role in this history. There is a pending challenge in the near future. The final resolution of the rebellion depends on several factors that pose great risk and vulnerability.

The good fortune experienced by the Zapatistas and Indigenous communities is profoundly related to the changes happening in the Mexican political system and its capacity to negotiate on a new stage. Without a profound political transformation, broad dialogue, and a reform of the state—something that goes beyond simple legal changes—the regional problem cannot be resolved.

As such, the new course of this transition, the consolidation of a new regime and rule of law, and the fortune of the movement that shields the insurrection, largely depends on the final result of this unpostponable and necessary change (Garcia, 2002: 302-303).

Among the changes that occurred after the shift in power in Chiapas last year, it seems that the governor is not leading an offensive against EZLN as his predecessors have done, but rather, the governor displays a prudent and respectful attitude. This does not mean his allies share this restraint (as they have delved themselves in disputing territorial control), nor that their development projects in the conflict zone or support for the Puebla-Panamá Plan are seen as an attempt to break down civil resistance among rebelling communities, despite their declarations (Hernandez, 2002: 21).

It needs to be clear, we must first obey ourselves. The powers of the Republic cannot act unilaterally—be it a chancellor or a president. They have to respect the capacity of other powers in this context—whether referring to trips abroad, economic openings, or international policies. This will strengthen the Mexican government and the entire country. This discipline will expand our political livelihood. This is what the Zapatistas have precisely called governing by obeying (mandar obedeciendo) (Montemayor, 2002: 22-23).

The Chiapas conflict has structural causes. The relationship that society establishes with Indigenous communities is rooted in a history of domination, erasure, and dispossession dating back to the conquest. The interests of the conquistador, like those of dominant society, are the appropriation of strategic resources such as water, land, biodiversity, and oil, for transnational corporations and the state.

We are talking about a history of submission and resistance, speculation and exploitation, that stretches from conquest to rebellion—a historical formation that can still be seen in the faces of the men and women who walk defying fate and who also find themselves representing a diversity of perspectives and experiences as the creators of new spaces in which the daily encounter with life, work, and the study and dissemination of conflict, quickly transforms itself. "As neoliberal politics provoke the deepening disintegration of the social fabric, in Chiapas and in the rest of Mexico, the organization of the people continues, in addition their efforts to reconstitute themselves as such and value their culture and identity, all of which is rooted in the defense of territory," affirms Magdalena Gómez, a lawyer and specialist on the rights of Indigenous peoples (Bedoya and Coon, 2014).

What actually happens in Chiapas is part of a more alarming situation: conflict between groups in power, organized crime, the consolidation of powerful groups that defy the law in order to satisfy interests relating to extortion and violence, the presence of new power structures with national and international networks, and the collective action in defense of territory and the self-determination of Indigenous communities.

It is within this new context that strategies emerge to build a just society from the conscious participation of communities and an organized civil society.

3.1 The Sociopolitical Situation: The Need for Change and Historical Struggle

BELOW IS MY TRANSCRIPTION OF A PANEL I PARTICIPATED IN ABOUT THE CHIAPAS SITUATION ON OCTOBER 7TH, 1996, which sought to reflect upon the process in Chiapas and the construction of relevant alternatives in the years after the emergence of the EZLN. Nonetheless, I do not believe it is possible to recover the moment: a confluence of different aspects flowing towards social and political transformation.

There are many general aspects that we may consider regarding the situation experienced by communities. There is a lasting set of problems that have been studied at the root, and that continues to be the reason for struggle among communities. In this process of struggle we must understand the origin of the social movement. Communities mobilize due to their own recognition of the problems they face. Understanding the causes of marginalization and oppression underpins the whole process, from which there are countless possibilities for action. In communities, lines of thought are developed through assemblies, workshops, meetings and the ongoing discussion that accompanies daily organized labor in communities.

A few elements to consider to understand the context of communities:

a.   The actual situation in communities and the urgency it has for them generates a movement toward action when we reflect as a community with a desire to transform it.

b.   The consideration of social and political conditions at the local level, local bosses, and mechanisms of control.

c.   An analysis of the structure of domination seen through the struggle for land in opposition to the interests of landowners and the state apparatus of provincial and federal governments.

d.   An analysis of the government model and linkages that serve to control Indigenous and peasant organizations.

e.   The economic analysis of poverty as a product of inequitable relationships and suffering created by the mechanism of international debt and extraction of wealth from Chiapas.

f.   Analysis of the neoliberal model that brings together the aforementioned elements and places them within a concept of a project of death.

On the other hand, there is also the conceptualization of the status of women, the interpretation of dependence, and the patriarchal system. There is a vision of the Indigenous world which emphasizes culture, rights, Indigenous peoples' autonomy, and the history of resistance towards the construction of a vast refuge for all. There is also the concern of finding explanations for the concrete situations characterized by marginalization, delays, corruption, injustice, the defense of the interests of powerful groups, the lack of expertise, and education.

These thoughts are found in the fundamental divisions that we find in communities. Each thought is sustained by the practices and the organizational processes that have already transpired. When a practice is delegitimized, the interpretation of reality and organization that sustain it are also delegitimized. Different organizations active in communities are constantly adapting to these three elements, which is why it is an unequal process. When a community group does not agree with the interpretation or practice, it looks to join another organization or create a different one.

One aspect of this differentiation is found in the relationship to the state as a whole, from which emerges the degree of independence compared to official institutions. Another element that determines this difference in organizations is in their connection or alliance with what the EZLN represents.

To the extent that organizations have succeeded in developing clear strategies, the discussion and mechanisms of unity, relationships, and alliances carry a different weight. This happens principally through the state assembly of the people of Chiapas, the transitional government of rebellion, the organizations that sustain autonomous processes alongside the EZLN, and the programs and counterinsurgency strategies of the military at the state and federal level. This becomes more complicated, however, with the stance taken by different political parties and by the presence of the church.

The design of these two strategies is very simple, but in some ways, it helps to identify the tendencies of organizations—the strategies for social change and the strategy of counterinsurgency—that in some areas develops into a war of low intensity where forces for violent confrontation manifest.

The combination of local economic and political interests among powerful groups with that of organizations underpins this dynamic. Nevertheless, civil society, the organizational strength of communities, and an urban population engaged in social change, grows as a space for non-militarized civil expression—although this is not confined to forces that are not represented in a consolidated organization. In other words, an organized community and civil society can be considered a new organization in contrast to old structures and longstanding organizations in power and those with ties to the government.

Organized civil society has the potential to build new relationships between people and communities, but can also be limited by the space that other organizations can offer. In Chiapas, as in other states in Mexico, there is a clear territorial limitation that corresponds to organizations. Given this, organized territorial control allows for an exercise of power.

In this sense, we can talk about two phenomena: that of division and that of confrontation, both of which are ongoing and long lasting. In this context, institutions function and group themselves around forces with which they can coalesce. For example, one cannot discuss the dangerous situation in the northern region of the state of Chiapas and defend human rights without taking a position, without putting oneself at risk at the hands of armed forces, that represent opposing interests. At the same time, one cannot act in isolation and independently in this process of confrontation.

On the other hand, the strategies built by communities transcend that of these very institutions and in some way, make it possible to move forward. In this way, we can understand all of the processes of unity and the quest to strengthen grassroots movements. The strategies are:

a.   Organized economic labor is part of the process that communities undertake in many ways to claim ownership of their own resources. They build capacity to improve their alternatives as they interact with society and take advantage of new tools, markets, and relationships between communities.

b.   Although much ground still has to be covered regarding the prior point, we cannot see it solely as development; this progress contains the need for change and a vision for a possible future, thereby gaining strength in the communities that work every day within an organizational process of production and commercialization, while attending to urgent needs and addressing state and regional development.

c.   This base of organized labor constitutes the network through which a myriad of activities are sustained and on which the meaning and potential of actions depend.

d.   Another strategic element is the search for unity, exchange, and the strengthening of social organizations at different levels. Reconciliation is a major focus in order to avoid confrontations and clashes within communities. This is possible through social movements and involves the transformation of institutions serving social processes.

e.   The concept of Integral Human Development, together with ethical elements in defense of life, constitutes the contributions of organizations and coincides with the proposals of communities.

f.   Another element is the demand for scientific work in the construction of society, technology, economic models, efficiency, and programs, as well as the demand for strategic planning.

g.   Strategy must come from reality. This is why we need to consider the conditions of communities, the present conflict, and security factors, as well as the danger posed by the existing conflict. At the same time, part of this realism implies considering this region within the strategic interests of the United States and the world economy.

h.   Solutions must be found in the future models that work to create progress and not regression. One example is the issue of land, which cannot be seen as part of the ejido[3] design but rather a solution that integrates elements of productivity and organized labor and engages as many workers as possible. On the other hand, today's problems exist within a generalized crisis while simultaneously playing a part in their resolution. The solution is a restructuring that must deal with all who are part of the problem. The fundamental and strategic element is a new society with new relationships. Therefore, the new world must be imagined and created with the vitality of those who are committed to that task.

i.   The path is open. We must secure our place in the future so that our task is integrated into that other time and within that process. Therefore, we must remain committed on a global scale. It is no longer about needs that are satisfied unilaterally with regard to education, health and employment, but rather it is about a new construction at the regional, national, and global levels; therein lies the value in generating a strategic action since each action and resource can be carefully oriented in the direction of that strategic goal.

j.   When we talk about economic initiatives, we're talking about productive processes that relate to strategic goals. The task is about carefully identifying actions and relationships so they can advance within the dynamic of the new society, with all the elements needed for them to manifest. The reality and the strategy demand actions that respond to these societal dimensions. From there emerges the responsibility for global transformations. This path is primarily taken by young people, as well as men and women with experiences with struggle and organizational work. Both unite around the same demands. When one walks with a strategic vision and within the dynamics of transformation, there are no roadblocks; for this reason, economic alternatives are also political.

Within the goal to create a new society with universal participation, there is the process of constructing Indigenous peoples' autonomy and the need to respect their culture. This comes with a process of development that belongs to the country as a whole. Furthermore,

---

3   A form of communal land that is federally owned but accessed by local communities.

it is related to Table 1 of the San Andres dialogue about Indigenous rights and culture, and the Indigenous forums that have taken place. In this way, the concept of autonomy has been consolidated and clarified, which, in turn, is connected to the peoples' inalienable rights to territory, culture, and self-determination, as well as justice and democracy in terms of the integral development of communities, and without isolating or establishing themselves as peoples living in conservation zones.

In Chiapas, the exercise of autonomy is present in the regional government, with its own authorities, laws, and regulations that command territorial control; these are called autonomous regions. There are also behavioral norms that identify each region, such as authorities and centers of reference that emerge as part of a process of an autonomous government and the ordering of organized civil society.

Indigenous peoples, their cultural past and their history of struggle are the foundation of this autonomy. Their strength comes from their roots, but their significance and political weight comes from their location and the strategic dynamic of the new society. In addition, certain autonomous mechanisms can be identified, such as the control of ruling groups or chiefdoms, which, in turn, can be interpreted as autonomous processes within the defense of economic and political interests.

Therefore, we face a complex, varied, and global reality, which has multiple interpretations and possibilities. Because state interests also possess this quality, it involves a long process. Militarization, in its own right, can be explained due to geopolitical and economic interests of the state. As such, the strength of the people is committed to the construction of a new society.

Here, I turn to José Saramago to illustrate a profound vision created by someone who is caught off guard by the circumstances at hand, yet confronts them with bravery and rage at humanity's suffering, while resurrecting each day with hope, like a flower in the desert.

Every morning when we awake, we may ask ourselves what new horror has been prepared for us, not the world, of which he who is poor is only a patient victim, but rather those who are our equals, humans. And each day our fear is fulfilled because humanity, which invented laws to organize life, also invented, in that same moment or perhaps before, the perversity of utilizing these laws for personal benefit and above all, against others. The human, my relationship, our relationship, patented cruelty as a formula to create exclusion on the face of the planet and from the perversion of cruelty has organized a philosophy, a way of thinking, an ideology; that is, a system of domination and control that has brought the world into the sick situation in which it now finds itself.

May this long preamble be useful to explain the state of mind I was in when I received the news of Acteal's massacre. We've been told "forty-five dead in Chiapas" since before there was talk of "insurgency in Chiapas." One accepts what is announced as if one was hit by a mallet, just another hit to add to yesterday's and to tomorrow's, another notch in the rosary of crimes committed by humans. Nevertheless, the morning when the news about the Acteal massacre was published, my home came to a stand still. We said: we have to understand. We have to share. And we went to Mexico, to Chiapas, to the center of the pain and to the heart of our past, to the only place where knowledge could be created. We went to Chiapas and we saw ourselves reflected in the eyes of Indigenous people, survivors of history's massacres, in the black eyes of mutilated children, in the incomprehensible patience of the elders that observed us, maybe even wanting to also understand. As we saw Chiapas' Indigenous peoples, we uncovered new countenances to the logic of power, the same as always, always unchanging across time, generations and their political uses.

We were in Chiapas. We saw the homes of Indigenous people, the displaced camps, the provisional settlements and those that were considered permanent. We learned their proposals for the future, that to them will always be imperfect, and that are reflected in the San Andres Accords that the government agreed to and now does not want to respect, and we met Rosario Castellanos, the writer that despite being dead for the last twenty-four years is still an ambassador for Chiapas, because in her novels she was able to tell the vicissitudes of the Indians and the violence of White people. We saw the Mexican army wearing military gear equipped to begin a war. We saw international supporters helping undernourished children and young women that had lost their teeth and their bodies broken like the dried clay that supports their houses. We saw poverty, the humiliation, pain, but we also saw the dignity in the words of the guerrilla fighter that would describe to us why he decided to rebel and back the call of the Zapatista Army for National Liberation, the last and perhaps only resource to curb the slow genocide suffered by Indigenous peoples in Mexico and the rest of America.

Because the Indigenous peoples in Chiapas are not the only ones who are humiliated and defeated in the world: on all five continents, alarming and criminal situations against groups, ethnicities, communities, and always the poorest of the poor, against what the prevailing the system, the authoritarian capitalism that runs the world, considers useless for its objectives, disposable, a toll, collateral damage that can be eliminated with no consequence; where the real perpetrators never pay, as we have seen again and again.

Nevertheless, in Chiapas, people have had enough. Indigenous peoples have organized to fight and negotiate. Alongside Subcommander Marcos, they have stood their ground against the government and have taught the world a lesson in dignity—and this is not rhetoric. The firm decision to live another life is felt in the men and women we have talked to, in the firmness and steadfastness of their actions and words, in the new understanding that they have of themselves. Indigenous peoples have taken on the responsibility of the Zapatista project, and as zapatistas, in other words, under the banner of "land and liberty" that Zapata wielded, they will continue to fight government, the latifundio, capital, and the idea of history that considers them superfluous, a species to be extinguished .

We went to Chiapas, gathered impressions, knowledge, and sentiments. We shared the pain and tears, like those who have come before us and those that will come in the future. We know that we have the obligation to tell what we saw, to say the names of the children, of the supporters, of those who became Indigenous to feel the way that Indigenous peoples have felt, and thus better understand. We carry with us their names: Jerónimo, Pedro, María, Ulises, Samuel, Marcos, Rafael, Ramona, Rosario, Carlos— Spanish names for an ancient and contemporary people.

Chiapas is not a newspaper headline, nor the daily dose of horror. Chiapas is a place of dignity, a spotlight of rebellion in a world that is pathetically asleep. We have to keep *going to Chiapas and speaking about Chiapas. They ask that we do. They say on a sign that is on the way out of the Polhó refugee camp: "When the last of you has left, what will become of us?" They do not know that once you go to Chiapas, you never leave it.*

This is why today, we are all in Chiapas.

(Saramago, 1998)[4]

Chapter Four

The Alternative Model

Creating a globalized world without neoliberalism has still not necessarily yielded an alternative that emerges from the common good of the planet. The change of values from an axis that starts from private interests towards another that points towards the vitality of the whole is not so easy, since it requires a strong change in values.

Globalization from below, aimed at the common good of humanity, constitutes a utopia that allows and supposes mass participation. However, the popular sectors are more disjointed than in past decades. In the midst of the flexibilization of the workforce worldwide, especially among the unskilled workforce, the organization of work through unionizing has lost much of its force. The globalization of the labor market globalized the replacement of the labor force. The subsequent organizational withdrawal of the workers can be seen, however, as a turning point towards a new organizational era. A global restructuring of unions is slowly brewing. It is no longer enough to organize at the national level, but it is necessary to structure networks around the transnationals, wherever they are, in the North and the South. Unionism has not died, but the objective conditions are in place so that a solidarity world citizenry capable of holding the transnationals accountable is is structured around the axis of transnational investment. (Dierckxsens, 1998: 77).

4.1 Dispossession and Land Defense

WE KNOW THAT CHIAPAS IS NO PARADISE, DUE TO THE DISPOSSESSION OF PEOPLE OFF THE LAND AND THEIR LIVING CONDITIONS. Interests in strategic territorial resources such as mines, rivers, oil, and agricultural production are affected by large projects of productive reconversion and the promotion of planting with transgenic seeds. In this way, new economic forces establish control through territorial dispossession related to the global, energy, financial, and environmental crisis.

In addition, impunity, the enrichment of officials, municipal leaders, and state authorities stands out. This is observed in the same families that have remained in power, inserting themselves in the structure of different political parties. Similarly, the disintegration of the communities, the division and the confrontation of the different power groups are part of a counterinsurgency war and the organization of crime. Therefore, the consolidation of powerful groups strengthens their organizational capacity to confront the established political power structure—legitimately or illegitimately. In this way, it could be said that we are witnessing the institutionalization of new power structures.

On the other hand, you can see in communities the depletion of resources, dispossession, disputes over territory, evictions, weakening, precariousness, deterioration in living conditions, hopelessness, migration, repression, threats, and abandonment of land and community. There is a tendency in communities towards division, confrontation, and pulverization. Young people, for their part, live in conflict with this situation.

Conflicts over land arise where there are valuable natural resources such as water, mines, wood and energy, which are called strategic resources because of their importance. Large companies have an interest in these resources and therefore want to appropriate these lands, whose value is very important for the entire economy of the country and the world.

Therefore, defending the territory implies that it does not become a commodity. When we perceive conflicts over land in our communities, we must analyze and discover what are the national and international interests that cause our quarrels. Behind the interest in strategic resources, there are those who see the land as a business: businessmen; municipal, state, and federal governments, which change the laws to be able to privatize the land; the military, the police, who defend the interests of the government; international governments, which seek to do business on our lands; and international organizations such as the UN, with its programs that seek to end poverty but do not respect or defend the rights of the communities.

In conflicts over the lands of our communities, our autonomy is attacked in order to stop the people from fighting in defense of the territory and to keep the land in the hands of national and international interests. Therefore, those who fight for autonomy also organize for the land to be protected by Indigenous peoples.

Those who defend neoliberalism want land so they can buy it, sell it, and squeeze its resources to enrich a few people. According to the archives of the Fray Bartolomé de Las Casas Human Rights Center, these are some trends of the land and territory problem:

→   With the arrival of *PROCEDE and FANAR,*[5] the land is put on the market. Thus, the law favors large investors.

→   Faced with an economic crisis, people go to pawn shops and seek out loans and/ or private equity holders. The demand for payment of these civil and commercial obligations will increase the dispossession of goods and land.

→   The dispute over natural resources (water, land, forests, minerals, seeds) will be intensified through projects such as the reactivation of mining, tourism, and ecotourism development.

→   The dispossession of the territory for hydroelectric projects will continue.

→   The case of Chimalapas generated conflict, which was resolved through the creation of new official municipalities on previously communal ejidal lands that belonged to the community members of San Miguel and Santa María Chimalapas.

5   PROCEDE is a World Bank endorsed program that is implemented by the Mexican federal government that sought to establish private property rights among individuals who use land under the *ejidos.* FANAR is a program that seeks to engage all remaining *ejidos* that were not part of the PROCEDE program in the process of privatization.

→ The dispossession of Zoque territory and the desire for its resources.

→ Since 1951, there has been a dispute over 41,418 hectares of territory on the border of Chiapas and Oaxaca.

Likewise, the REDD+[6] forest program is an example of population and territorial control. In addition, currently 60% of the grains consumed in Mexico are imported, which represents a serious risk for food security.

It is also believed that the EZLN will defend the ownership of lands recovered in 1994. As such, conflicts to possess the land will increase between organizations, communities, and peasants—each with their own tendencies, militancies, or political support.

---

6   A UN backed program that is described as attributing financial value to the carbon stored in forests and offers incentives to reduce emissions from deforestation and land degradation.

4.2 The War Path

ACCORDING TO THE FRAY BARTOLOMÉ DE LAS CASAS HUMAN RIGHTS CENTER, population and territory control persists in the country via operations in accordance with United States' war manuals, such as that of militarization, paramilitarization, and counterinsurgent strategies.

The United States government and the Northern Command create the necessary conditions to open the war front on the southern border. In June 2011, the Central American International Security Conference was held with the representation of the governments of the United States, Mexico, Central America, and Colombia. With this, three military plans were established in the region: Plan Colombia, the Merida Initiative, and the International Conference on Central American Security, with a total budget of $6.4 billion dollars (USD).

Within this context, the Mexican military base was integrated, with at least 24 agents from the DEA and the CIA, and retired commando troops from the Pentagon's Northern Command. On the other hand, in Chiapas two new military bases were installed, one on the Comalapa border and the other in Pijijiapan. These actions were meant to adjust the territorial model of use of land, subsoil, water, and forests, as well as the tangible and intangible heritage of the communities, to the requirements of capital. This was done using fear, the displacement of the population, and an increase in attacks on autonomous projects, thus continuing the destruction of the social fabric to fragment community resistance.

At the same time, community members are being criminalized, accused of protecting drug traffickers and/or guerrillas, while sacred spaces and ancestral customs are altered. This situation causes forced migration to safer places with better economic income.

The offensive against those who organize and speak out extends to the civil population at large and, in a particular way, against indigenous peoples, alternative media, and human rights defenders. As a result, the territory is cleared and left vulnerable to investments in mining, tourism, biofuels, monocultures, rural cities, and national and foreign electricity generation.

4.3 Mesoamerica Project

IN JUNE 2008, DURING THE TENTH SUMMIT OF THE TUXTLA DIALOGUE AND AGREEMENT MECHANISM, in the city of Villahermosa, Tabasco state, Mexico, the presidents of nine countries signed the Villahermosa Declaration. There, they proposed the transformation of the Puebla Panama Plan (PPP) into the Mesoamerican Integration and Development Project or Mesoamerica Project, with the aim of improving the quality of life of its inhabitants.

With this new name, a new impetus has been given to the PPP, always under the same logic: to integrate and prepare the regions stretching from southern Mexico to Colombia under the mandates of neoliberalism, in order they serve big capital (Mesoamerica Project Exploitation and Dispossession of Mexico to Colombia, 2011: p. 4).

The confrontation of models is present today. The strategy of the neoliberal model is to claim, use, and deplete natural resources around the globe. The concentration of power implies the use of weapons, political pressure, information, and control of territory; that is, economic, political, cultural, and social control.

We are faced with a global reality that modifies national and international structures, the defense of rights, and the legitimacy of decisions. Likewise, we are witnessing a global, energy, financial and environmental crisis, which places us before the fall of an economic and corporate model established with the logic of territorial dispossession and the depletion of resources.

The construction of an alternative model comes from the socio-political practice of communities. The roots of this confrontation run deep and are present in the pained cries of freedom and the understanding of the nature of things.

On the other hand, when traveling the roads of Chiapas, one can observe the different transformations of the landscape, the proposals to overcome poverty, the abandoned programs, the infrastructure for development, such as a communal store, a drinking water system, and municipal agencies. New homes have also been built, more roads are opening, and vehicles are able to transport goods, however, rocks and warehouses that store wood appear where there were once forests.

The inhabitants of the communities, especially youth and women, work on the plantations in the north. In addition to this, the pace of violence and confrontation have increased, as has the struggle for interests and unlimited profit. This context creates a perceived loss of purpose, confusion, abandonment, and hopelessness.

This is the new landscape, where states undergo a very rapid transformation process. The reality of communities is permanent change, so that inoperative formulas remain in the past and new proposals arise.

At the same time, it is clear that an isolated response cannot give consistent results. A set of actions with a certain logic is needed to achieve outcomes that can mark progress. What is happening now is the confrontation of different development models.

The State proposes a development model based on the strengthening and accumulation of wealth by transnational companies, which prioritize the appropriation and dispossession of strategic resources from peasant and Indigenous communities. This approach emphasizes the need to find a solution to population growth and to marginalization as an isolated phenomenon, which has become radicalized in the face of the global crisis. Therefore, a strategy of militarization and accumulation without measure, ethics, or future is perceived.

These types of proposals come from an individualist perspective, which seeks partial solutions to marginalization, unites religion and the economy, and advances towards a prosperity based on occupying new sectors—such as transportation, commerce, lumber, coal, and labor trafficking—that arise alongside new populations.

Another issue with the traditional power model is how it maintains control over resources and the population, and exercises political, cultural and religious power through traditional means. These powers defend themselves against the new leadership of the communities while expelling dissidents and maintaining a powerful control over the community in political and economic terms.

In the last 40 years, an alternative model of struggle for land and political participation has provided a useful context for the exercise of autonomy. This, in turn, has generated a peasant-Indigenous movement to lead agrarian struggles against repression that have shaped Chiapas. This movement, now fragmented, has created a space for independent organization, which has the ability to negotiate with the government and exercise regional power to make it possible to defend its interests against the development model of the State.

Finally, there is the EZLN's proposal, which is based on a process of building autonomy, i.e. an awareness and political practice of resistance to the imposed model, while explicitly defending the land and collective rights of Indigenous people and peasants. This proposal has the capacity to function as a strategic organization with a concrete vision of political interests, which are nurtured by experience in the struggle of communities. It promotes the exercise of autonomous power in autonomous municipalities. Above all, it has the ability to assume responsibility for creating alternatives, while considering the need for a change in the structural relations of domination and dispossession in the communities.

4.4 The Fundamental Elements of an Alternative Model

The Social Subject and The Organization

Through the organic process of constructing groups, organizations and complex networks are established that share a common methodology from their inception. This process responds to objectives and interests of the social subjects which are ultimately the product of this alternative model to domination.

Land, Location, and New Spaces

The land is the deepest essence of space and nature. The appropriation of the land, knowledge, defense, and the fact of constituting itself as part of a territorial reality is the result of a new consciousness. Therefore, it is not about the struggle for land, in agrarian terms, but about a vital space to build communities and societies. The land births new spaces with the ability to transform the environment and create conditions for subsistence.

Strength, Awareness, Information, and Knowledge

The construction of a force which provides people and communities with the capacity to maintain their pursuit of long-term strategic objectives is a task that is achieved with realistic awareness of the situation. This awareness is the product of knowledge accumulated by historical experience, work, suffering, research, and the ability to resist; it is a vital and dynamic knowledge enriched with the information and data acquired in exchange, study, dialogue, and sincere community reflection.

Praxis, Local Work, and Collective work

Praxis is the concrete relationship from which all relationships emerge, and in which the relationship with the global can be experienced. Collective work opens the possibility of building alternatives and structural changes; it is the permanent action towards a social construction for all. Collective work represents working together to achieve common goals. Being organized within a collective entails responsibility and the practice of common ownership of the means of production, which is experienced in decision-making and in the contributions of the capacity and ability of each participant.

Responsibility, Autonomy, and Spaces of Power

Autonomy is the capacity to assume responsibility. Moreover, it seeks to clarify a system of relationships to achieve consensus based on the well-being of the community. It symbolizes the emergence of a social subject with the ability to lead the actualization of the community in an integral way. This subject has a broad vision of the relationships necessary to establish regional, national and international development processes, thereby ensuring the product of experience and that actions have continuity and are directed towards strategic objectives.

Resistance and the Ability to Build Solutions

Resistance is understood as the act of rebelling, eliminating dependency, and excluding mechanisms under the terms of the State, which is primarily responsible for dispossession and accumulation. For communities, resistance represents the ability to decide for themselves and exercise that right.

Solidarity Economy

Solidarity economy is organized production, based on the understanding of resources in relation to the local, national, and international market. The requisite recognition and appraisal of this economy includes: knowledge, research, planning, administration, training, learning, technology, legal forms, economic resources, communication, and efficiency. Likewise, this economy arises from the action of social subjects as organized entities, which constitute the strength of communities by maintaining creative and responsible actions.

This economy produces and is based on solidarity, as well as equitable, reciprocal, respectful, and interchangeable relationships between communities and people. It is a plural exercise in creativity, as well as the search for inclusive alternatives for the autonomy and self-management of communities.

Coexistence

The ability to recreate spaces and achieve dreams while living fully is attained through coexistence and its alternative forms, such as participation in political parties and the ability to express our "gift of people." This makes it possible to establish relationships with the past and the future and to align with different movements of the universe, people, and communities. It is in these spaces of traditional dance, food, and drink that we deepen our presence in nature.

Constant Change, New Relationships

The circumstances that produce changes within an ongoing confrontation are:

→   Autonomy and resistance.

→   The sense of dignity and justice.

→   The defense of community organization and culture.

→   The promotion and protection of human rights.

→   The construction of popular power.

→   Integration into the global market.

→   The disintegration of the traditional agrarian community.

→   Political and military control.

Dialogue and Respect

The process of building a new society implies participation, exchange, dialogue, respect for the opinions of others, plurality, a complete vision thanks to universal participation, and the search for unity in diversity.

Historical Memory

There are many elements to historical memory: recovering history; escaping oblivion; becoming a society with a past and a future; recovering events so as not to forget them; and learning about the sense of time as spatial continuity, as an origin and a future.

Networks and Articulation

Articulating the work of networks allows an understanding of a broadly connected space with different centers of power and confluence, a diversity of actions and a real and concrete occupation of a global territory. Individual contributions are combined with other contributions to produce results for the common good.

The Structures

The structures are the tools that must correspond to the model as a whole. They are norms, mechanisms, principles, institutions, the guaranteed right for communities to coexist, and the resolution of conflicts.

Energy Sources

The first source of energy is found in nature, plants, and animals. In this way, we must all discover and create the paradise where we live.

Another source of energy is ourselves. Each person is a source of energy, since we have a body with mobility, awareness, feelings, thought, the ability to learn, and will. However, you have to learn to build such power.

The third source of energy is society, since all men and all women exist in historical and cultural continuity. With this energy, the construction of organizational processes arises to produce just relationships between people and communities.

The fourth source of energy is God, divinity, spirituality or the life of the spirit.

Building Peace

We need to renounce the interests of capital, profit, commodification, militarization, and security strategies based on weapons and the most powerful threats. We need to resist entrenched power, humiliation, utilitarianism, competition, oppression, mechanisms of repression, and the establishment of control systems through fear. We must build paths of freedom and give something of ourselves to achieve peace. We must also take responsibility for situations that destroy coexistence and the right to life, as well as renounce violence in the strict sense of destruction and denial of life. Building peace builds systems of equity, participation, affirmation, distribution, and collective property.

4.5 Zapatista Autonomy as an Example of the Alternative Model

WHEN THE STRUGGLE STARTED IN '94, we initially fought for eleven points, which would later become thirteen (land, housing, work, food, health, education, independence, freedom, democracy, justice, peace, and lastly culture and information).

The thirteenth came to be after the San Andrés Accords. We were not sure how we were going to achieve it, but now we are seeing how. We imagined that a lot of food or doctors and hospitals would arrive, but we did not imagine that we and our own children were going to be the doctors, the architects, engineers, and teachers, who were going to teach us. We did not imagine that we were going to create an autonomous municipality and that we were going to have Councils of Good Government (José Luis, Autonomous Council, 2003).

Autonomy is an alternative to the colonial society model. It is a way of organizing against power relations. As an example of this long-term construction, the Sixth Declaration of the Lacandon Jungle of 2005 is presented, in which reference is made to the autonomous Zapatista rebellious municipalities.

Well, we begin to put our effort into the autonomous Zapatista rebellious municipalities— that is how the communities organized to govern themselves, to strengthen themselves. This mode of autonomous government was not invented solely by the EZLN, but comes from several centuries of Indigenous resistance and the Zapatista experience itself. It's similar to the self-government of the communities. In other words, it is not that someone comes from outside to govern, but that the people themselves decide, among themselves, who and how they govern. And if these leaders do not obey, they are removed. In other words, if the one in command does not obey the people, their authority is stripped and someone else governs.

Then we saw that the Autonomous Municipalities were not all on the same level. There were some that were more advanced and had more support from civil society, and others that were more abandoned. In other words, it was necessary to organize them more evenly. We also saw that the EZLN, with its political-military faction, was getting involved in the decisions that were up to the democratic authorities, to "civilians," one might say. Here, the problem is that the political-military part of the EZLN is not democratic, because it is an army. We saw that it was wrong for the military to ascend in place of democracy. The military shouldn't decide what is democratic. It must be the other way around. That is, democratic politics commanding from above and the military obeying from below.

Or maybe it is better that there is nothing below, where everything is on the same level, without the military. Well, but then, from this problem, what we did was begin to separate the military from the Zapatista communities' autonomous and democratic forms of organization. And so, actions and decisions that the EZLN used to make were gradually passed on to the local, democratically elected authorities. Of course, it is easier said than done. In practice, it was very difficult. It took many years to prepare for war, in a context where the military government had also become strengthened. But we did it anyway, because we mean what we say. If not, then why make statements if we aren't going to follow through?

This is how [...] the Councils of Good Government were born in August 2003, and with them the self-learning and exercise of "command by obeying" continued.

Since then, the EZLN was no longer involved in giving orders in civil affairs, but has accompanied and supported the authorities democratically elected by the people. Furthermore, they ensured that the communities, as well as national and international civil society, were well informed about the support received and how it was administered. And now we are passing the work of monitoring good government to Zapatista support bases, with temporary, rotating positions so that everyone learns and carries out that work. Because we think that a society that does not watch over its rulers condemns itself to enslavement, and we fight to be free, not to change masters every six years. (EZLN, 2013: 223-253)

Autonomy cannot be established without resistance to domination and control mechanisms established by the capital system, which subjugates and dominates in order to appropriate strategic resources and accumulate wealth in local, national, and international power groups.

Zapatista autonomy is part of the EZLN's strategy to build an alternative to global capital and global domination, since both are illogical without a neoliberal model. Therefore, the Zapatista autonomy is anti-capitalist and seeks to build an alternative model to the neoliberal capitalist system. This implies overcoming conflict. In other words, it is a construction of peace that corresponds to the future of humanity.

Constructing an autonomous social and political force with alternative, equitable, fair and ethical practices is the future. Permanent change is achieved with an alternative model.

On the other hand, there is no longer the traditional agrarian community in which a common identity prevailed. Resources existed for well-being and subsistence, and the authorities and socio-political structured allowed for the regeneration of communities that were somehow considered isolated and marginalized.

Nonetheless, we are currently heading towards the construction of a globally integrated community, in which each element is broadly contextualized in such a way that a local event has to do with a broader issue. That is, the situation of a community is contextualized within a larger global issue.

The alternative to the neoliberal model is built by communities, through their work, thought, organizational forms, collective work, culture, and vision. Thus, the hope of humanity lies in the construction of a new paradigm that continuously renews life without reproducing the current system of power.

In order to understand the new paradigm, it is important to consider that we are facing a difficult situation in the local, national and international context, which affects our lives, our families, and our sense of the future.

Today, we are entering a new paradigm. This means that a new form of communication with the totality of beings and their relationships is emerging. Obviously, the classic paradigm of science continues to exist with its famous dualisms such as the division of the world between material and spiritual, the separation between nature and culture, between human being and the world, reason and emotion, feminine and masculine, god and world, and the atomization of scientific knowledge.

But despite all this, due to the current crisis, a new awareness of the planet as a whole is developing. From there, arise new values, new dreams, new behaviors, assumed by an increasingly growing number of people and communities. It is from this prior awareness that a new paradigm is born, according to T. Kuhn. It is still in the gestation period. It has not been fully realized. But it is giving the first signs of existence. A new relationship in dialogue with the universe is already beginning (Boff, 1995: 29).

4.6 Building a New World

CONSTRUCTING A NEW WORLD AND AN ALTERNATIVE SOCIETY IS PART OF THE EFFORT OF ZAPATISTA AUTONOMY. It is about making progress in the relations of production, the collective ownership of the means of production, lifestyle, expectations, capacity, and the methods and mechanisms to resolve conflicts. Proposing the strategies of "commanding by obeying" and "walking in query" help explore solutions and growth.

In this alternative society, it is important to consider the significance of women's participation and their rights. In Revolutionary Law of Women of the EZLN, the following notions are put forth:

→   Women, regardless of their race, creed, or political affiliation, have the right to participate in the revolutionary struggle in the place and to the degree that their will and capacity determine.

→   Women have the right to work and receive a fair wage.

→   Women have the right to decide the number of children they can have and care for.

→   Women have the right to participate in community affairs and hold office if they are freely and democratically elected.

→   Women and their children have the right to health and food.

→   Women have the right to education.

→   Women have the right to choose their partner and not be forced to marry.

→   No woman may be beaten or physically abused by relatives or strangers. The crimes of sexual assault and rape will be punished.

→   Women may occupy leadership positions within organizations and achieve military rank in the revolutionary armed forces.

→   Women will have all the rights and obligations mandated under the law.

In this way, work, study, training, organization, structures, workplans, and an awareness about the conditions that we currently experience are required. The process must also be similar to the growth of plants, which is ongoing yet imperceptible.

Therefore, the task of building a new society belongs to everyone; it is not just a task of Indigenous peoples. It has to do with being responsible subjects and participating in the construction of alternatives to power structures that deny people's dignity, subjugates them, deprives them, and imposes societal models.

Some necessary elements in the construction of autonomy are:

an awareness of one's own history,

equality in difference,

labor to change relations of domination,

the equitable distribution of work and goods,

collective work,

the input of women and men,

respect for nature and ourselves,

agreements,

collective purpose,

collective participation,

non-violence,

resistance to war,

democracy,

justice,

and dignity.

The power of Zapatista autonomy is that individuals have rights. In this lies the permanent hope and the anarchistic act that is built and defended through the power and will of communities.

The demand for autonomy by Indigenous people in Mexico has been met with a neo-Indigenist governmental action known as neoliberal multiculturalism. This governmental response is a series of calculated changes in the legal and institutional order that mark a continuity of government actions masked by a rhetoric of change and the acceptance of a Pluricultural Nation. However, these legal amendments which ignore the possibility of recognizing Indigenous autonomy, have been answered with the implementation of "de facto autonomies," situation that leads us to position this debate from the point of view of its promoters, from the way they propose and implement their autonomous project, from what they imagine, and what they expect from Indigenous autonomy, beyond what legal and institutional changes can offer (Cerda, 2011: 31).

The fundamental challenge is constructng an autonomy in the face of what the government dictates, which consists of forcing us to maintain and conform ourselves to the small spaces and precarious conditions in which we live. In other words, they do not want us to question the state, given that it belongs to them, government officials and the powerful, ruling elite. However, Mexico belongs to all of us since we are Mexican—in addition to our particular identities. For this reason, we all have a responsibility to participate every way possible in the construction of Mexico.

When we speak of land defense, we refer to collective territory, that is, the motherland, which has historical roots. There are thousand year-old aspects of autonomous construction, such as considering oneself part of the universe, a perception that leads indigenous peoples to make land defense the basis of autonomy.

We have to look at history, know where we come from, what we are made of, what the root is of what we are now, understand our bodies, understand ourselves in this space and time, each of us with our own strange quirks, but within the landscape that guides and defines us. We must be aware of the blows, the wounds, the rebellions, the resistance, the history of domination and the emergence of consciousness, the experience of freedom, tenderness, respect and love.

We need memory to fight openly, walk the paths of freedom, avoid deception and lies, understand the past, launch ourselves into the construction of the future, establish continuity for the construction of everyone's house, and see memory as the basis of rebellion. In this way, the dimensions of what we are and what we seek are understood.

Our existence is a collective, communal and transcendent existence, not in the sense of appropriation of resources, but in the defense of resources for humanity. For its part, autonomy is linked to the transformation of exploitative relations and resource depletion.

Zapatista autonomy is related to the construction of an alternative economy to capitalism, i.e. a solidarity economy. The base of the economy is the territory with all its resources. The autonomy of the people is attuned to resistance, liberation and permanent construction. In this way, autonomy consists of the responsibility we assume to create spaces of freedom, with the capacity to transform relationships of subjugation, establish solidarity actions to grow, and act collectively to be strong and not repeat the past.

Within the great complexity of local, regional, national and international relationships, it is important to know the power of local actions, anarchistic acts, and the new worlds created in community. Collective work is the fundamental element for the construction of the solidarity economy, as well as the process of autonomy.

Therefore, Zapatista autonomy is the space for free, responsible citizens—builders aware of the challenges that correspond to them as part of a community, an ethnic group, a state, a region, a country and the world. Assuming this global responsibility is the option against neoliberalism, which generates necessary conditions for the emergence of alternative models of society for everyone.

Now, I will return to Immanuel Wallerstein to highlight the perspective of social change towards an alternative to capitalism, which is necessary to achieve an equitable distribution of goods and an egalitarian society:

Liberals have always asserted that the liberal state—reformist, legalistic, and somewhat anarchistic—is the only state capable of ensuring freedom. And perhaps that was true for the relatively small group whose freedom it safeguarded, but unfortunately that group has never moved from a perpetual minority to becoming the majority. They have always continued to assert that only the liberal state could guarantee a non-repressive order. Critics on the right have said that the liberal state, in its reluctance to appear repressive, allowed or even encouraged disorder. Critics on the left, for their part, have always said that in reality the main concern ot liberals in power is order and that they are quite capable of repressing, only partially hiding it (Wallerstein, 2003: 4).

Now we have to see if we can create a very different world system, a system that includes everyone in its benefits [...].The final formulation of a clear antisystemic strategy for an era of disintegration will take at least two decades. All we can do now is propose some elements that could be part of that strategy; but we cannot be sure how all the pieces fit together, nor can we claim that the list is complete (Wallerstein, 2003: 246-247).

Living in a community can be a contribution to the search for other peoples, because it is necessary to find ways to live in harmony with nature, in peace, with justice and dignity. Autonomy is a need and task for society as a whole, not just for indigenous people or agricultural communities.

In Zapatista communities, there is a process of building autonomy that goes back many generations, beginning with the departure of the Indigenous peasants from the farms where they lived and worked as servants. In this way, these communities have advanced in the construction of autonomy from the social, political and ideological aspects. Therefore, it is about the construction of a transformative mass movement that resists the strategy of annihilation by the established power.

The construction of autonomy is born from an ancestral decision regarding the relationship with the powerful, the government, and the mechanisms of submission and deception with which those with power act. Likewise, this construction is based on the knowledge of these conditions, on history, the body, and one's own experience.

Another fundamental element for the construction of autonomy is found in the conscious decision to participate in work, organizing, training, study, discipline, collective efforts, step-by-step learning, and recognition of what is possible to get done. Similarly, having your own time is an individual and autonomous decision.

Thus, the perspective of autonomy is global; it is the search for freedom for all of Mexico. At the same time, autonomy requires universal participation. Without it, autonomy will not be built. The fight is of and for all the people of Mexico. From there arises the need to convert autonomy into a practice of civil society, since therein lies the essential qualities of Zapatista autonomy: justice, democracy, and freedom for all. It also corresponds to the ethical exercise that guarantees respect for privacy, rights, and a dignified life for people, i.e. a democracy that guarantees freedom and justice.

Governing ourselves leads us to self-determination and the appreciation of the collective rights of communities. Likewise, the collective rights of communities are part of human rights. Therefore, it is important to recognize the collective rights of communities in relation to the territory; strategic resources for life; and their culture, language and identity, ways of life, security, communication—which is established through community radio stations.

In the face of wars of domination and extermination, it is important to learn to resist. Resistance is also a way of building alternatives.

To resist is to identify the reason why you are going to fight, to resist is to fight in defense for land, it is to fight in defense for education, health, housing, work—that is what it means to resist, because in the the moment you are fighting you are resisting and feeling the pain of others.

To resist is to not be apathetic to that which affects your compañero or your compañera, because that is what keeps us firm, if we hurt togther. Because I can grieve for my daughter, I can grieve for my family, but if I see a brother who is having a difficult time, or I see a sister who is carrying a malnourished child, that motivates me and commits me to something larger, and that is resistance. I will resist for you because it is not fair that being able to live a dignified life we have to accept this life, that's how I see it (María Trinidad Ramírez, member of the People's Front in Defense of the Land).

We have to learn to overcome conflicts between people and communities, which makes it necessary to learn to overcome violence with practices of construction of collective reason and common paths to freedom. But how do we conceive this collective being made up of everyone? Therefore, we will continue fighting and we will do so with a clear struggle in our conscience.

Therefore, this struggle will be long-term and its central purpose will be the construction of autonomy. We have to stop war by building peace and autonomy. Justice, democracy and freedom are also processes that we must all undergo. That is why we need to join our forces, our hearts, our say in alternative acts to the mechanisms of power which deprive, humiliate, lie, deteriorate, and destroy the structures in which life grows.

The self-conception of the EZLN as an armed movement that struggles to conquer civil spaces to create a political platform for all Mexicans, has constituted an important challenge for indigenous movements: to leave behind their local and regional isolation to approach civil society from a global perspective.

If the EZLN responded to paramilitary violence, the state would justify the use of military force to take over Zapatista territory and thus stifle the autonomous experience.

It was thought that the Zapatista experience would succumb over time. The truth is that although it decreased in visibility, it consolidates its autonomy and serves as an inspiration to ethnic groups that promote similar processes.

4.7 The Process of Building an Alternative Model

IN THE NEW ERA WE ARE LIVING IN, WE HAVE THE TASK OF BUILDING A NEW HOUSE FOR EVERYONE. To do this, we need to make a very important decision, which will separate us from the past. Broadly speaking, one of the essential elements of this construction is the creation of collective subjects with an awareness of the reality in which we live, taking into account our bodies, minds and hearts in order to reach our potential and the realization of who we are.

We are community, family, society and multitude, and to understand this dimension of ourselves, a change of attitude is necessary, a personal conversion towards the community to learn to be together; it is a form of spirituality that sets the pace for us to walk together.

The strengthening of collective subjects depends on their organization, operational capacity, the resources they have, the options available to them, the direction and intentionality of the actions, their experience and mobilization, the understanding of reality and knowing how to place themselves in the local, national, and international context, and taking action in different historical and political conditions.

Collective subjects must foster a dialogue with the world, be in solidarity, establish respect as a fundamental part of the exercise of freedom. This means promoting communication as a strategic action to achieve an understanding of the different ways of seeing, feeling and acting. This must be a peaceful, comprehensive, and profound exercise which will allow the construction of social, economic, political, cultural and spiritual alternatives to avoid war and build peace.

The construction of these alternatives is based on the collective ownership of the means of production: action, production, knowledge and consumption of healthy food, as well as the equitable distribution of goods, gender equity and respect for diversity, taking into account the limits and the new ways of relating in a broad and global dimension.

Strategic action allows us to consider the need for security to defend life and to carry out conscious and responsible actions. Therefore, the struggles for justice, resistance, autonomy and the construction of a social and solidarity economy are a priority, and this requires generosity, delivery, donations, and communication.

We need an ethic that requires us to take care of the universe and respect life, and guide our actions in the defense of the land, seeds, biodiversity, and different values. We must maintain historical memory, the memory of a project for life against a project for death. The construction of an alternative power and project with its own timeline is required in order to globalize hope.

People Moving Forward Together

What follows is for all of us to move forward together along the path of responsibility and work. The important thing is to have a position and the political understanding to think and act—without it, there will be no direction because there can be no action without an understanding of the context.

Structures for participation, creation and change are needed; that is, a movement capable of changing the situation is required. The exercise of rights, for example, is a practice. The important thing is to identify the change and see where its force is heading: how is this force growing? Where is it going? What elements constitute this change? How are we going to join this path? Are we going to strengthen ourselves with these changes? What should be our attitude, work and transformation?

It must be a faster and more radical change, which includes the whole of the people and the whole of the person; those who have the desire to change, but must also change many things. Nobody wants to stay stuck where they are, doing the same job. Therefore, openness and strength are needed to change. And for this, it is necessary to be willing to work to achieve the great historical, broad, and lofty dream in which the presence of free women and men who walk with high spirits is appreciated as light.

All of the above, Oaxaca, Guerrero, campaigns, and the efforts of many people are worth is, as is their birth, youth, energy, love, responsibility, cry, shouts, thoughts, feelings, common and collective work, and production for each and everyone. It is a huge effort, but it is worth it.

We will walk together so that there is no suffering, so that justice appears in our home and so that there is no loneliness. We will not stop doing what is necessary, we will not give up work. We are going to feed on this energy, strength, capacity and imagination. No one should be left behind. We need the hands, the heart and the imagination of each and everyone. This is the plain that we have conquered and which we are establishing for our future…and walk in this great plaza with firmness, determination and creativity; meeting others to dialogue and opening our doors and windows in the path of the wind.

Now, what can we do to transform reality? Interpret reality, be honest, peaceful, look into each other's eyes, walk learning and open our hearts. And what do we do? Learn from our resources and get closer to them so as not to lose their energy, work in an organized manner with joy and happiness, encounter nature, be willing to change, learn and think together.

Some references on the diversity of processes in the world can be found in the Intercontinental Network of Social Solidarity Economy (RIPESS, in its Spanish acronym) and in the Network of Social and Solidarity Economy (REAS, in its Spanish acronym). In these spaces we can learn more about the path of building the solidarity economy and experiences such as food production, free systems, and health management. We will also learn about how the collective ownership of the means of production is organized and their relationship with nature, land and the subject.

The Vision of the Future

We have a great accumulation of experiences and knowledge of the past and present, which is a social synthesis that drives us to keep walking. From that position we can build a new world, which will be shaped as a movement that will go beyond the thousands of displaced people and refugees of this time. Each group of displaced persons or refugees must be a symbol of resistance, which motivates the creation of new social relationships beyond subordination, discrimination and exploitation.

To build the future, we have to be aware that we are building people power through our own capacity to build a new society—we do not have to ask permission from any authority. It is an autonomous action exercised only by those who have the capacity to build.

All over the world new groups are emerging with the clarity of building an alternative to the neoliberal model, a new way of living. We observe the emerging force of humanity, which finds its salvation in the sources of life.

Challenges for the Future

Creating alternatives requires the necessary discipline to consciously act on the main contradictions, in order to survive. This implies knowing how to recognize and position oneself in service of peace within a context of war. It also means having the ability to analyze issues and understand how important it is to have a broad vision of the world in order to integrate local experiences with global initiatives.

The challenges for the future require the use of appropriate technologies and tools, civic participation, openness and dialogue, and the construction of plural participatory structures. They also require the ability to move forward and generate something new and beneficial for all, creating ethics and law that prevail over the material benefits of development. This implies building peace and fighting against the use of the military in national and international conflicts.

Strategic Elements for the Future

land   biodiversity   plurality   universal rights   the rights of women

the rights of the people   self-determination   autonomy   resistance

the equitable distribution of assets   participation   popular power

an alternative solidarity economy to the neoliberal model

10 Steps to Approach the Future

What are the tasks of this stage?

1. **Become stronger.** Be self-aware, know your strength and capacity. Find the seeds of freedom within us. This is a personal task that no one else can do for you.

2. **Work together.** This path is not a competition. Tolerance, dialogue, consensus, organization, and discipline are needed.

3. **Discover what life will always have to offer, without focusing on transience.** This will help us to have the necessary strength for the long haul.

4. **Be caretakers of life.**

5. **Overcome obstacles.** The path of building alternatives is full of obstacles, therefore we have to learn to defend ourselves to overcome what is put in our path.

6. **Walking consciously.** Thinking about how to walk through darkness without slipping; to analyze the interests behind the obstacles.

7. **Build.** It is a creative activity based on our vision of the future.

8. **Produce.** It is about producing knowledge, encouragement, organization, work models, food, goods, ceremonies, anarchistic acts, peace, conscience, consensus, and strength.

9. **Transform.** It corresponds to transforming ourselves, going from passive to active, from consumers to producers of our food, and from being the ones who obey to being the ones who also rule.

10. **Distribution of goods.** What we produce, build, and transform should not be for the few, but for all. Therefore, it is not about making more wealth for some, but sharing goods—forests, water, air, land, happiness, joy and peace—for there to be justice.

Fundamental Elements of an Alternative Model

The social subject, the ensemble, organization, and collective word

Territory, location and the new spaces

Strength, consciousness, information and knowledge

Practice, local work, collective work and collective action

Responsibility, autonomy and spaces of power

Resistance and the capacity to self build solutions

Solidarity economy

Shared living, celebration, participation, commitment and the gift

Constant change, new relatinships, strategies, rights, dignity and justice

Dialogue and respect

Historical memory

Networks

Structures

Energy sources

Chapter Five
How to Construct Solidarity

Solidarity Economy is built through practice. Individuals and social movements expand and acquire a real presence in society within the framework of mobilization and social activation processes by large strata or sectors of the population, which sometimes undergo profound transformations as a result of their own activity (Razeto, 1993: 25-26).

In August 1991, the magazine *Encuentros* published a reflection of mine entitled "After Analysis," which had the aim of showing the need for a strategic sense of the transformative action of exploitative social relations.

To act more clearly, we need to take into account several elements:

1. We Live in an Economic System against the Culture of the People

There is no solution to domination. There is no effort to address the cause because the people are considered a reserve army of cheap labor.

Within the modernizing project, the people have no other prospect: they are the labor force for foreign investment and they are also the basis for legitimizing power. This is going to be well observed in the elections.

2. Do Not Lose Sight of the State At All Levels

Understand what the state means, what constitutes it, which is not just the government. The State includes repressive forces (police, army), the media, political parties, peasant and worker corporations. It also has an ideological apparatus, a culture of domination and dependence that surrounds the people and demands that they assume the behavior that corresponds to a dominated entity, i.e. accepting the conditions of the system.

The State has the power to solve problems, this is the constant messaging. The State also has a great capacity to be heard, to convince, to control and repress. To that end, it uses multiple resources and different methods.

To understand it, it is important to analyze the role played by law, credit, general concessions to support production by the marginalized, caciquismo, the role of corporations, etc.

3. Historical Patience

The most permanent part of the system in which we live is the economic structure, the relations of production, relations of economic domination. Chiapas, for example, in the last decade of the twentieth century, is a large farm and the mechanisms of labor exploitation do not change even though there is TV and the landowners drive the latest car models.

This leads us to locate the present as the product of a historical process. The current system has been around for a long period and is part of a set of broad relationships at the regional, national, and international levels. At first glance we do not see these fundamental forces that reinforce it; one vivid way of expressing this can be the image of an ancient tree with many leaves and deep, extensive roots. It will not be easy to cut because it is reinforced on all sides, despite its roots not being visible.

Thus, it is necessary to have historical patience, since things cannot change immediately. However, we must remain active in building conditions for change to occur, even if we do not see immediate results.

4. Those Belonging to the System are Organized

They have power and they want to stay in power. Their system knows how to repurpose opposition. Its capacity is such that it uses the opposing force to its benefit. It has managed to convert the demands of the people into leverage in order to legitimize its power, managing the needs of the people (see Pronasol) and thereby "defending the rights of the oppressed." This leads us to think about how an independent organization can be manipulated and used.

For this reason, it is important to advance the process of organizing communities with the notion of defense in mind. We shouldn't carry out these processes if we cannot defend them, because they will be dressed up in the logic of the established power. We must not let them rob us of our power, which is our only source of wealth. For the power of the State, it is better to rob us of people power than money.

5. Become Aware of Freedom

Freedom is not free, it implies struggle. Freedom is not conferred in some kind of act, it is earned in the process of struggle. In this process, the intentions of the one who dominates are discovered along with spaces that remain to advance their conquest.

The space that can destabilize the system, despite a permanent economic base and the political power of the State, is the space of conscience—the ability to fight for freedom, the understanding of workers as managers of history. A solid will that can confront the mechanisms of domination and the relations of production that constitute the economic base of the system.

Therefore, the unity of peasants, workers, and students is necessary at the local, regional, national and international levels. This broad awareness unifies the workers. This will be the force capable of taking on the system. This is the long-term hope, with a strong sense of history.

A new culture is needed, with a notion of life based on the struggle for freedom and an awareness of what freedom is; new activities, relationships, and spaces for culture. We must establish principles of new life: hope, solidarity, desire for freedom, elements of collective struggle, and the ability to join class projects, in a broad sense, without borders.

We must fight against language, against subjugating acts, and attitudes of domination. Hence, it is important to take the time to understand myths and ideologies, the bonds of consciousness. You have to work in these small spaces defending yourself from manipulation and creating conditions for freeing actions; as well as strengthening ourselves by making complete decisions and accepting the consequences that arise from them, since it is a collective, not isolated struggle.

Learn to speak, to say your piece, to listen, to defend the notion of equality, but also to question it against the reasons of others.

Our project of change must therefore coincide with practical models that generate freedom. What is needed are people capable of fighting for freedom, those who seek out life with the capacity to fight, to build against what is built and defend themselves from the dominant powers.

5.1 Elements to Consider When Constructing Political Solidarity Economy

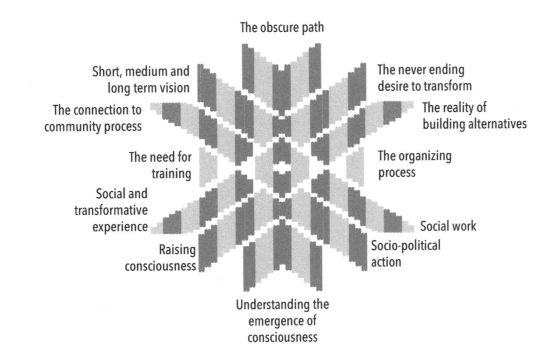

The obscure path

Short, medium and long term vision

The never ending desire to transform

The connection to community process

The reality of building alternatives

The need for training

The organizing process

Social and transformative experience

Social work

Raising consciousness

Socio-political action

Understanding the emergence of consciousness

Elements of Training

→   The personal journey

→   The space for transformation

→   Society's model

→   The world

→   The system

→   Responsibility

→   Our time

Elements of Local Action

→ Culture

→ History

→ Identity

→ Solidarity

→ Origins

→ Local movements

→ Solidarity processes

Elements of Local Action

→ Strength in diversity

→ The conditions of collective action

Elements of Industrial Action

→ The state control over communities

→ Action within the system

→ Criminalization of social action

→ Repression

→ Institutions

→ Structural interests

Elements of the Social Subject

→ Collective action

→ Awareness

→ Collective property

Global Challenges

→ Local power and global power

→ The construction of global citizenship

→ Decolonization

→ Participation of the people

→ Peace

→ Production

→ Reproduction

→ Solidarity

→ Land and territory

→ Transformation of conflicts

→ The necessary transformation of life

→ Life as nature, environment, land, air, water, heat, germination and biological diversity

→ Energy sources

→ Egalitarian relationships

→ The interests that exist toward strategic resources

→ The anarchistic processes

→ Strategic resources

→ Refugees and displaced people in the world

Elements of Alternative Construction

→ Knowledge and its construction

→ Exchange

→ Anarchist thought

→ Decolonial action

→ Communication

→ Creativity

→ Generic diversity

→ Gratuity

→ Participation

→ Production

→ Collective property

→ Responsibility

→ Utopianism

→ Our personal roots

→ Networks

→ Egalitarian relationships

→ Other worlds

Political Solidarity Economy as an Alternative to the Neoliberal Model

→ Learning

→ Dance

→ Universal well-being

→ Exchange

→ The market

→ The construction process

→ The collective subject

→ The individual who builds political solidarity economy

→ Territory, resources, and land

→ Employment

→ The abundance of resources

→ Collective action

→ Autonomy

→ The search for comprehensive achievements

→ The ability to build solutions

→ Building power

→ The defense of life

→ The distribution of goods

→ Diversity

→ Transformative energy

→ Celebration

→ The purpose of production

→ Identity

→ The refusal to become commodities

→ Organization

→ Participation in management

→ Plurality

→ Collective ownership of the means of production

→ Concrete reality

→ Resistance

→ Society at large

→ Technology in service to the community

→ Truth

→ Purpose

→ Ethical principles

→ Strategic processes and resources

→ Value

Elements of the Journey

→ Alternative movements

→ Alternative worlds

Strategic Elements for the Future

→ Popular power

→ The land

→ Self-determination

→ Autonomy

→ Biodiversity

→ The alternative construction to the neoliberal capitalist system

→ The equitable distribution of goods

→ Participation

→ Plurality

→ Resistance

→ The rights of women

→ The rights of the people

→ Universal rights

Visioning Elements

→ Creative imagination

→ The vision of the future

Elements of Exercise of Freedom

→   Detachment

→   Escaping structures of subjugation

→   Keeping spaces open

→   The realization of potential

→   The historical memory of anarchist paths

→   The process of building alternatives as an exercise of freedom

5.2 How Do We Construct Solidarity?

THE PRESENT SITUATION IN THE WORLD HAS LED US TO NEGLECT. Although, at the same time, it has led us to recognize what we have learned and our potential.

Therefore, we have come across a long path where we can go forth and do what we are called to do: the construction of an alternative model for the current system in crisis. I believe that we can choose which way to advance and where to place ourselves so that our actions contribute to a new society, towards the new human; or rather, towards authentic human beings who transform relationships of submission, subjugation and inequality.

Responsibility

Here is a list of a series of principles that outline responsibility:

1. To take matters into our own hands.

2. To reject that which mistreats, dominates, subjugates, humiliates, weakens and places us in desperate circumstances, makes us dependent, and hinders our capacity to make decisions, and be individuals or communities with history and culture.

3. To reject the bare minimum, control, fraudulent mechanisms, government bureaucracy by those who dominate us so they don't have to justify their mechanisms of power or give them permission to advance their strategy for domination and control.

4. To not be passive and naive people who surrender their status as have-nots against the haves who have accumulated wealth and power based on deceit, lies, and war.

5. To step into this power by negating it, neutralizing it, and taking away its opportunity to establish itself.

6.   To reject being dominated with our own resources.

7.   To take responsibility for building alternatives.

8.   To own our path.

9.   To work together.

10. To construct our liberation.

11. To foster awareness of our own responsibility.

12. To construct our position before the State and government.

13. To not be silenced.

14. To not allow our rights to be denied.

15. To understand the government's strategy behind new proposals for "Rural Cities", "Opportunities," and "New Dawn."

16. To know what is really happening.

17. To prioritize the dignity and beauty of our proposal. The political solidarity economy is a collective process.

Seven Ways of Understanding Current Views On Solidarity

Building solidarity is urgent and necessary, since societal interests instruct us to deny it. Therefore, it's important to understand it in opposition to dominant trends.

The seven elements that help us understand solidarity are as follows:

1.   Collectivity as a fundamental element to construct a society of fulfilled people in the face of individualism.

2. Cooperation, not competition.

3. The valuing of people and nature in the face of hyper-commodification.

4. Respect and dialogue with nature and all living beings against dispossession and the destruction of nature.

5. To share, exchange, and receive the equitable distribution of goods against the accumulation of wealth and power.

6. Collective property against individual property.

7. To support the right of citizen participation, rather than denying of people's rights, dispossession, humiliation, or subjugation.

In sum, we will continue walking. Although there are many challenges, we can do something. We have the tools and knowledge to achieve our objective. We can recover a part of the historical experience of our people and ourselves; we can begin our own adventure.

We have to learn from the present moment through our participation and our longings. Let us recognize the power of solidarity to construct free men and women. Let us reflect upon the idea of property: everything belongs to us in some way and we can take responsibility for everything. To live in solidarity, we must be in service to the world. Without that, it is impossible to build alternatives to the deterioration of the system and the society in which we live.

Chapter Six

Relationships Within Political Solidarity Economy

6.1 Economy and Collective Work

AN IMPORTANT MOMENT OF REFLECTION ON POLITICAL SOLIDARITY ECONOMY TOOK PLACE DURING THE FIFTH (2005) AND SIXTH (2006) SOLIDARITY ECONOMY MEETINGS in San Cristobal de Las Casas with representatives from Mexican and Guatemalan communities, along with people who shared their experiences from other parts of the world.

Collective work benefits everyone; but organizing ourselves requires effort and time. There is a need to unite; create networks; walk together; exchange knowledge; share ideas and capacity; take individual responsibility; expand consciousness; and acquire more information on the benefits of collective work. This work is for the benefit of families and communities.

Now, we split into two distinct realities. The first corresponds to the present economy in which there is an efficient and competent organization. In this way, communities experience constant dependency, the general power of exclusion emerges, and people are repeatedly used as objects to generate profits.

The second reality is found in solidarity, in which planning contributes value to internal solidarity, demonstrates that we all matter and have the capacity and recognize the value of one another. This creates a spirit of consciousness, fraternity, and self-esteem within each person.

On the other hand, within the scope of complex local, regional, national and international relationships, it is important that we discover the immense potential of local actions, liberatory acts, and new worlds, as they are created with everyone's help. In that way, collective work is the fundamental element of the construction of the solidarity economy and, in turn, the process of autonomy among the people.

Currency

Money is an important factor because it represents us during transactions. Nevertheless, it does not mean everything to us in the solidarity economy. Money is useful when it is used well, and so it must be seen as a tool. Conversely, it brings with it problems when it is used poorly or mismanaged. Money shapes us more in urban areas where it fosters crime, unsafe conditions, unequal trade, devaluation, and control by the powerful.

Without money, we look for another mode of survival. In medicine, for example, medicinal plants can be used in the absence of economic resources. In the same way, political solidarity economy does not require money. We can trade, barter at the local and regional level, supporting each other in different places and producing various goods for consumption without having to buy them.

Money is tied to everything. This is why when we analyze our communities, we connect the political solidarity economy with this mode of exchange. Our ancestors and our forefathers used money sparingly, as they practiced bartering and also produced healthy organic foods; this is to say, they ate everything Mother Earth produced without the need for money.

Development, Growth, and Distribution of Goods

We would like to replace the type of development that has created death, yet we are at a disadvantage. The new development model we want via political solidarity economy must break with the notion of money and competition. We want a type of development with dignified conditions for education, health, housing, attire, and nutrition for all people of the world; in which vital human growth and harmony with families and communities are established.

This new development model establishes harmony with the earth, nature and communities. It seeks equity and justice among men, women, children, elders, and young people. Community work is personal. It involves family and community development through capacity building that supports human beings achieving their own autonomy.

Technology

The first thing that comes to mind when we think about technology are the machines that are unavailable to us, in other words, the ability to technify our activities to obtain better benefits and a common good. However, if the masses come together, many ideas can emerge and results can be achieved with greater benefits and less effort.

Political solidarity economy and technology form part of a change in thought and attitude that comes from capacity building. In this way, we use technology to produce common benefits and work happens organically. This change is brought about through organized work. Nevertheless, there is much still to do, such as advancing work done with the hoe and the machete, rather than using chemicals, and rescuing the way our grandparents lived.

Our knowledge and the way in which men and women organize is part of technology. Women's craft work and the way they organize to advance this work is technology.

The Emergence of Social Subjects

Social subjects form to the extent that people are able to build an alternative to the neoliberal model. In whichever form this takes, new transforming subjects emerge. The fundamental wager is in the creation of collective subjects, both critical and creative; in other words, builders of alternatives through collective work and organized in a continuous relationship of thinking, feeling, and working to construct through praxis and not only as a byproduct of overthinking.

Democracy

Critical subjects taking action against a system of domination by building alternatives to the neoliberal model will result in a just society with a capacity for collective decision-making. It is the foundation of an autonomous process with shared responsibility of the reality and conditions for all. This includes overcoming violence and war; establishing a democratic society in the truest sense—not only in the search for consensus, but through the capacity of collective action, plurality, and diversity among harmonious subjects in the struggle.

An exercise in democracy must coincide with political solidarity economy since the process of producing and distributing goods is a fundamentally political act. Because of this, it seems to me that it is important to return to the concept of "mandar obedeciendo" within Zapatista communities, which is understood as complex representation and consultation, and in acts of collective decision-making that orient the global task of education, health, and production.

Also, I would like to refer to the book *The Little Zapatista School and The Contagiousness of Autonomy* by Jérome Baschet (2014), which speaks about the experience of the little Zapatista school: "The descriptions given during the little school seem to invalidate a purely 'horizontal' reading of *mandar obedeciendo* as the absolute predominant expression of the assemblies and decision-making power equally assumed by all" (16). Through his own reflections, maestro Fidel invites a more complex reading of the work:

> *There is a moment in which the people rule and the government obeys; there is a moment in which the people obey and the government rules. It is evident that 'mandar obedeciendo' departs radically from the power relationships that the State constitutes, that even when there isn't electoral fraud, it remains a powerful mechanism of disposession of collective decision-making and the consolidation of the status quo by 'experts' made up of the political class and bureaucratic machine (Baschet, 2014: 16).*

Autonomy

The wealth we have as a community corresponds to our biodiversity, lands, traditions, work capacity, organization, and wisdom. We know that we are very capable. To that end, we must defend our rights in the face of government plans. We must build our own strength; use the resources within our community in the process of production and research its different applications to strengthen our collectives.

We think that autonomy is the best way to organize ourselves, since we cannot do anything without it. With autonomy, collective efforts for justice, democracy and freedom are valued. Autonomy encompasses many things, including many peoples, each with their own culture, language, collective work, and organizing style. Autonomy encompasses nature as well.

When we speak of autonomy, we not only do so for our own communities, but for all the peoples of Mexico. In Chiapas, for example, people talk of autonomy, in Guatemala of local power. Both are more than a dream; it is about a goal involving *compañeros* and *compañeras* to achieve autonomy and the construction of freedom, justice, and memory within Political Solidarity Economy.

Autonomy must be achieved collectively, through family and the people, based on their needs and pooling our resources while attempting to recover memory through processes and traditions. Autonomy is the responsibility of work done in service to the community. It looks to create new worlds, new ways of living with one another. Learning and praxis, in this sense, are a positive outcome of the political solidarity economy, which has as its economic base that which is constructed through the exchange of goods. Autonomy is the end goal, but to reach it, political solidarity economy is required.

The base of the economy resides in territory and its resources. The strategy of the neoliberal model is the appropriation of resources, as well as their use and exhaustion. The concentration of power taken for granted in this strategy implies the use of weapons, information, political pressure, and the control of territories, i.e. economic, political, cultural, and social control. Therefore, the social movement must resist, create, construct, analyze, and act.

The process of constructing the peoples' autonomy consists of resistance, liberation, and permanent construction. Autonomy is the responsibility we undertake to create spaces of freedom, transform relationships of submission, and establish acts of solidarity to grow and act collectively with strength so as to not regress into the past.

There is a correlation between autonomy and resistance; in this way, it is possible to resist if there is a capacity for autonomy and autonomy is possible if there is a capacity for resistance. The production and construction of an autonomous economic foundation resides in an exercise of resistance, as it assumes obtaining alternative goods, nutrition, health, education, a healthy life, relationships, and structures. To live, construct, be free, self-govern, and grow as a people requires resource-rich territory. As such, the defense of territory is very important, since without territorial autonomy, the rights of the people, and the economy, neither culture nor dignity can exist.

Food Sovereignty & Agroecology

We also cannot advance in our goals due to the scarcity of resources. We have requested support from the government but we have been ignored. Therefore, we choose to organize with our own resources, without the government's assistance. Our ability to product and the goods that different communities and regions offer is the strength with which we resist. This ability to produce and exchange our products is what gives us food security.

Agroecology is the organized work to regain the strength of the land, recognize the value of our resources and use techniques that conserve the land, trees, plants and all seeds. With this in mind, we seek to make the lands fertile, ensure that there is water, humidity, so we can live with all of the goods nature offers. With agroecology, we also strengthen the political solidarity economy; we seek to understand our Mother Earth to live together in harmony; we respect plants and animals because we share our territory with them.

Local, National, and International Markets

It is necessary to find markets where there is a great variety of products and people can respectfully engage with one another.

Nevertheless, small growers have difficulties with the market. And so, alternatives emerge, including the production of high-end goods, the diversification of growing plots, and the use of organic fertilizers to protect the environment. To highlight the importance of culture, there are crafts, high-volume production, and the preservation and rescue of traditions.

The system in which we live does not allow us to advance and sell our products; we find ourselves in an oppressive system. The problem for producers in the market is that products are practically given away. Therefore, fair trade that develops networks of commerce and local and regional fairs must be established. In this way, we could support each other and achieve better prices for our products.

Similarly, we know that earth's resources are running out yet we continue to use chemicals in an attempt to increase production; we have lost the way of work and culture, and so we must recover them for our children.

We we say 'other worlds,' we mean an alternative model of society, another manner of living, thinking, being, and doing. The alternative model is born from the necessity and the power of communities; it concerns a concept that grants the right to share and organize.

Today, there is a conflict between these two models: one comes from the strength of communities and the other is compelled by governments and transnational corporations. The neoliberal model, which enjoys every manner of resource and advanced technology, is geared toward the accumulation of wealth. The alternative model does not have financial resources or capital, but it possesses all the human resources needed: consciousness, capacity, solidarity with the people, and organization for the construction of other worlds.

It is important to deepen the conversation on the need for collective property, since it is one of the paths to ownership that can achieve the most unity among workers and a better distribution of wealth. With the practice of collective ownership of land, machinery, money, and technology; a better understanding of universal equality is possible.

The practice of political solidarity economy is a permanent impulse to change unjust relationships and transform prejudice, as it drives the peoples' knowledge and wisdom, which comes from the process of production, the understanding of nature, and all that happens in the lives of communities.This practice comprises the strength to break with the structures that dominate, humiliate, and subjugate people.

The political solidarity economy promotes the participation of men and women, as well as different ways of acquiring knowledge and individual capacity. This economy is also connected to the diversity of crops, trees, animals, production in all climates, ancestral knowledge of ancestors, and knowledge of the modern era in which we live; it also looks for the abundance and diversity of seeds, fruits, and people.

Gender and Women's Struggle

Gender is the role assigned to men and women at birth. When we say men and women, we refer to the idea that there should be equity in terms of respect and responsibilities between these genders.

Education resides in decoupling ourselves from the roles and assigned behaviors that are neither just nor equitable. The development of wisdom occurs through reflection. We are all complementary beings and have the same rights. Therefore, men should understand the rights of women and their worth. In this way, respect towards women is observed, as well as the participation of men and women.

Political solidarity economy is one of women's bases of struggle. Women's organized labor allows them to have their own resources and strengthen their group formation. Their shared experience allows them to see the world, understand it, and decide to fight to change the conditions that exploit and humiliate women.

In the organization of women, there is a struggle for their word to have the same value and for their work, presence and decisions, to be respected. Women are driven to stop violence against women and for all of us to be conscious of this situation. In this way, the struggle of women opens possibilities for universal freedom.

The Struggle for Self-Determination

The right to self-determination implies the struggle for territory, which is a strategic fight for the construction of an alternative model to neoliberalism, in which there exists the real and concrete possibility of a different mode of production.

We can approach this discussion from diverse perspectives, such as through experience and peoples' practices; ideas of autonomy and its relationship to production and the modes of production; the permanent exercise of constructing autonomy and the solidarity economy; the reconstruction of our cultures, subjects, spaces; and the fight for autonomy and against the imposition of neoliberal interests.

The fight for territory is for the peoples' rights, the defense of territory, and seeds. It is in favor of biodiversity and culture, and against transgenics and patents of our own resources in the hands of transnational corporations.

The fight for biodiversity is related to the basic notion of political solidarity economy in which it is possible to produce a great diversity of food by having a type of food sovereignty as a people and as nations.

The neoliberal capitalist system is in crisis because a system based on the use and exhaustion of resources cannot be sustained, nor can a system be sustained in which the accumulation of wealth turns everything into commodities, denies people's dignity and their rights; discriminates against indigenous peoples' cultures, and places women in an inferior place in the service of men.

Therefore, a system that destroys and wants to eliminate the sources of life cannot be maintained. The political solidarity economy gives us the possibility to have resources, foods, knowledge, organization, and the capacity to construct other necessary worlds.

Chapter Seven

Fundamental Elements of Political Solidarity Economy

IN RESPONSE TO THE SITUATION FOR INDIVIDUALS AND COMMUNITIES who suffer flooding, displacement, violence, death, losses and every consequence of deteriorating living conditions, the dimensions of the political solidarity economy appear as an alternative model to erasure, competition, and commodification.

The fundamental elements of political solidarity economy are arranged as follows:

The Root

The need for an alternative model is the root. We can visualize this model as a seed with all its elements to be developed.

Therefore, we see the political solidarity economy as a solution for all, based on collective participation, and constructed at the local level through local resources. This economy is the response from peasant and Indigenous communities to overcome the conditions of poverty and the economic, political, social marginalization in which they find themselves due in great measure to the structural and historic exclusion of the neoliberal capitalist system. Communities turn towards political solidarity economy when they expand their awareness of the reality in which they live, convincing themselves that the situation will change only if they participate actively and in an organized manner in the transformation of that reality—in other words, turning into the protagonists of their own development.

This social subject is strong. Its base and collective principle are the people and communities that become linked through solidarity with resources, consciousness, ideas, works, efforts, interests, convictions, capacities, and objectives to bring about concrete actions that benefit all of that collectivity. This social subject drives and constructs the political solidarity economy within communities through effort, ideas, and their own dreams.

Communities, for their part, choose self-realization for their own purposes. Consciousness, unity, and solidarity are therefore very important. It is about strengthening and constructing a community to reestablish it from a new perspective. In this way, mutual aid and solidarity cease to be things forced by circumstances and transform into conscious and necessary principles. In other words, collectivity is a conscious organizational process to change circumstances, and nothing new can be forged without these principles. To edify the new, respect of difference is needed, i.e. pluralism.

The Structure

The structure refers to organized communities, which constitute the collective subject that acts and generates transformative relationships, and forms an organization with the capacity to be present in the time that corresponds to it.

The Organization

Organization depends on the amount of people, knowledge, development of thought, creative and productive work, needs, resources, technology, objectives, and the expected results—in addition to what can be gained through experience.

The Practice

Practice is found in work, creativity, the capacity to make decisions and act, participation, experimentation, productivity, efficacy, solidarity, the understanding of needs, the distribution of goods, the exchange of goods and knowledge, programming, and the structure of a force built through collective energy.

Work is the activity that sets all the elements in motion; it is the path as well as the point of arrival; it is tied to the type of creativity that is observed when, for example, we take raw resources and transform them. Therefore, we could define work as an incomplete action, as each action leads us to another. To be receptive to this learning process gives our lives a sense of purpose.

On the other hand, there is an accumulation of energy that transports us to a different phase. It is a spiral that takes us towards something new, that expands upon our new circumstances and strengthens the alternative constructed by history.

Today, actions that began in the 1980s have a new dimension. These actions began with the idea to achieve a common good for the collective along with a clear understanding of what happens in the regional, national, and international context. In any case, they are now part of the construction of autonomy.

In the beginning, there was a desire for economic gain, but now, a change in lifestyle is required, i.e. working to transform unjust relationships and to transform ourselves as a people. With these two goals, political solidarity economy establishes a dialectic connection with all social relationships.

The work of peasant groups is born from the will to do something to meet their particular needs and those of the community. Will is created through the understanding of reality, aligning with community organizations, reflection, and analysis. Through collective work, commitment emerges; clarity comes through organization. As a result, processes are established through work relationships with other groups.

Continuity

The continuity between the political and the social, then later, productive labor, generates experiences from which new goals and strategies for struggle emerge.

Strategy

Strategy is the search for a better future, a new society, and a new world in the long term. Strategy anticipates a new relationship between the local and global, between what we are already and what we are yet to be. It is a kind of geometric growth, nonlinear, through which each grouping has its own potential and complexity.

These processes do not necessarily depend on each other to grow and may also act according to their own dynamic. On many occasions, those who begin a process become fatigued and do not wish to continue; nevertheless, their work can grow. Strategy resides in the present, given that in the work can be found the dreams of those who search for a change to the conditions of poverty and marginalization.

The Fundamental Tasks

The fundamental tasks consist of the creation of collective subjects starting with awareness of reality and incorporating our minds, bodies, and hearts. The strengthening of collective subjects depends on their organizing; operational capacity; resources; decision-making capacity; the direction and intentionality of actions; their experience and mobilization; an understanding of reality; knowing how to position themselves in the local, national, and international context; and the way to act according to different historical and political conditions.

The collective subjects find themselves in a type of dialogue with the world. The main focus of this dialogue relies upon the organizational capacity of transformative subjects, which consists of engaging in group relationships.

What occurs at the local level is the result of a combination of situations that is the product of our history. We must mobilize in a broader context, globally, and through the complex relationships which we are a part of, be that personal or communal; because we have lived revolutions, the experience of the nation-states, and that of solidarity.

We live in an expansive space, with multiple transformative processes, conflicts, wars, destruction, death, and the defense of life. Therefore, the fundamental element in the conception of civil society is the possibility of participating in the search for a new society.

The culture and peoples of Chiapas have existed for thousands of years and as such, have a great capacity for resistance and a will to grow as a people. It is about communities with deep roots in the past and a vision for the future, which belong to a more expansive context that spans Nicaragua, El Salvador, Honduras, Guatemala, Belize and southeast Mexico, and constitute a history of resistance.

These communities will not stop resisting for the most part because their capacity for resistance has grown within this context. A generation of this struggle has not been in vain since the resultrs have been achieved thanks to the recovery of autonomy, culture, the appropriation of space, relationships between communities, the vitalization of what it means to be Indigenous and have one's own language, the ability to establish networks, and the ability to survive. In this way, people live, enjoy, celebrate, and engage in rituals and creativity, despite military presence and the repression that exists in this country.

Solidarity has the same root for all human beings; it is born from the deepest consciousness and has the goal to permanently transform human beings. Since it does not have limits, it is built on experience, builds bridges of communication with all the peoples, strengthens the structures to make possible the sustainability of justice, dignity, freedom, exchange, knowledge, and self-discovery; it is a strategy for the future. Solidarity has to be expansive and global, such as the mechanisms of domination of the financial markets and goods.

Interconnected Peoples

Networks are indispensable structures in the construction of political solidarity economy because they imply the notion of a global and interdependent reality. At the same time, networks are the construction of an interactive civil society, capable of constructing alternatives for the public sphere that is open and participatory and that produces connections.

The political solidarity economy is the construction of civil society, beginning with collective political participation in the search for universal solutions. This formation is realized in practice; it is a process of constructing the subject as a whole, which is why it is necessary to know the experience of collective action. It is about a constant relationship between the wholeness of the being with its body, feelings, character, thought, future vision, interests, and political commitments. The realm of collective action is learned this way and not reduced to the local sphere. It transcends the meaning of action when incorporated into the actions belonging to the same strategy. This is why the multiplicity of actions produces transformation.

The collective subject constructing political solidarity economy is present in each act of resistance against domination, colonization, and in the construction of alternatives to the neoliberal model in any dimension. These are imperceptible acts, but, at the same time, they are powerful because they are part of a dynamic that is present in the world. The reflexive act consists in assuming this dimension responsibly and maintaining consistency so as not to destroy what has been constructed with effort and work.

Communication, Solidarity, Respect, and Freedom

Through a profound and complete exercise of nonviolence, it becomes imperative to stop wars and construct peace. It also becomes necessary to create social, economic, political, cultural and spiritual alternatives; manage collective ownership of the modes of production; take collective action; produce knowledge; cultivate and consume healthy foods; and distribute goods equitably. This must all be done while taking into account the limits and new ways of interacting in an expansive global context.

Strategic action encourages us to consider the need for security, to defend life, and to take conscious, responsible actions. Therefore, the struggle for justice and the construction of a political solidarity economy through resistance and autonomy are prioritized. This, in turn, requires generosity, commitment, giving, communication, collective work, praxis, and the conscious decision to do something collectively.

Relationship with Nature and Playing within the Universe

The relationship between nature and play within the universe corresponds to collective ownership, exchange, sharing, accumulated energy, the concentration of different processes and procedures, germinating seeds, culture, the realization of the true value of things, actions, symbols, the necessary time, the meaning of play in time, one's own time, spirituality, giving and receiving, recognizing the need for one another, recognizing the knowledge and values of others, art and poetry, the construction of knowledge, technologies and processes.

We are talking about strategic action capable of transforming reality and relationships of injustice; the rupture of relationships of exploitation and building the power to achieve peace, justice, and the distribution of goods. This is to say, we search for the construction of a singular force for the future, such as the manifestation of the power of the marginalized, the displaced, migrants, and refugees.

It is about creating a strategy to live freely, to love, and to be in solidarity; along with the intention to develop, find purpose in life and work, create goods, wealth, nature, society, and relationships. We need to globalize hope and put forth a global ethics that demands forms of care for the universe, respect life, and guide our actions in the defense of territory, seeds, biodiversity, and values, so that we can maintain historic memory.

Chapter Eight

Methodology

THIS CHAPTER IS INTENDED TO SYSTEMATIZE THE NECESSARY STEPS to achieve the construction of an alternative to the neoliberal system, whose base is found in the defense of strategic resources for life. The only way out of oppression is through the construction of freedom.

This is why it is important to try to relate with each group, person, or assembly: to foster rebellion, as part of a shift in consciousness or in creative capacity. Also, there must be an understanding of what rebellion against domination means, the self-determination of peoples, the dispossession of resources, the defense of territory, the practice of predatory capitalism, the construction of alternatives, the defense of territory, and self-care.

We need to become aware of what we have constructed and gained via this history of local, national, and international struggle. It is not only about a local process, but rather collective mobilization and what happens in each organizing space that constitutes totality. This is why it is important to not lose sight of different contributions and practices.

Now, the government crisis is critical, given that a systemic crisis has no ending and cannot reconstruct itself if it doesn't strategically align with society as a whole. In this way, there exists a serious division among the dominant classes—in addition to an exhaustion of the mechanisms of domination. Therefore, mechanisms such as deceit, manipulation, and the way leadership dominates in all spaces, cannot remain.

In this sense, there would need to be a delegitimization of the presence of the military, paramilitary groups, militias, intimidation squadrons; public relations and the use of media; authoritarianism; and patriarchal and misogynistic societies—in addition to the proven efficiency of laws, judges, prosecutors, and the police.

As we find ourselves before the crumbling structures of domination, it is time for creativity, *kairos*, and new life. This time and space is reserved for collective action to depart from existing power structures. We cannot turn back, we go forth toward new land and sky. This is not a promise, but a choice and a fundamental option for life.

On the other hand, it is true that change cannot happen through one action or mobilization. Life goes on. A prolonged action is not necessary, as individuals can become fatigued. Nevertheless, the next action must harvest the fruit of the prior action.

We also must not lose hope because we have yet to transform the system and our lives—what matters is that we are on the path to victory. We must continually ask ourselves if we are willing to construct alternatives and carry out the necessary work to reach our goal, with conscious focus on collective and political action.

In this way, it is not about putting the government on trial but about taking ownership over governance. It is the construction of the peoples' autonomy that comes with the experience of autonomy. They are no longer able to deceive us, as there exists an awareness among the people, as well as a sense of dignity and rights, and a clear position against the neoliberal model. We should appreciate having been born in the 20th century and being present in this process which began after WWII, when imperial capitalism was established and then became global.

We are more aware of human rights, autonomy, and civil resistance. As a result, the need increases for a government with a new national project that should defend the common good and protect the nation's resources from transnational corporations. The process of constructing a new society and a new government implies social, economic, cultural, and political changes; it is a profound transformation that must happen within the family, the community, and in the heart.

This change comes from civil society. It must manifest and work for a world where diversity and rights are respected; where there is food for all; and where justice, love, and peace are established. With the participation of civil society and grassroots organizations, it will be possible for a new government to respond to needs; prepare and direct the nation toward a model of society where people have dignity; produce healthy food through collective labor; and ensure health, education, employment, trust, and security. Furthermore, those who are in power must have an ongoing relationship with the people to construct a new society.

8.1 The Practice of the Political Solidarity Economy in Chiapas, Mexico

The Social and Economic Proposal of the Zapatistas

The practice of political solidarity economy in Chiapas has been strengthened by the autonomy established and maintained by the Zapatista Army for National Liberation (EZLN). The practice of resistance and the Zapatista peoples' autonomy have demonstrated with more clarity what political solidarity economy entails and how important it is for the defense of territory and collective ownership of the modes of production. In this way, the political solidarity economy is part of an expansive alternative model, i.e. an advanced system that is constructed from autonomy and the resistance of Indigenous peoples.

On the night of December 31, 1993, in the southeast Mexican mountains, the Zapatista Army for National Liberation took over the municipalities of Ocosingo, Altamirano, Las Margaritas, Oxchuc, Chanal, Huixtán, and San Cristobal de Las Casas, and declared war against the Mexican military.

El Despertador Mexicano, the EZLN's newspaper, compiled the Lacandona Jungle Declaration, the Law of Rights and Responsibilities of Peoples in Struggle, the Law of Rights and Responsibilities of the Armed Revolutionary Forces, the Revolutionary Agrarian Law, and the Revolutionary Women's Law—in addition to laws corresponding to urban reform, labor, industrial, commercial, justice, social security, and war tax.

Those who are marginalized and subjugated by the system rose up in arms outraged at the situation. They saw that a definitive struggle against oppression was necessary. This declaration of war is opposed to the destruction and death produced by neoliberalism; it is the defense of territory, emerging from the construction of individual will, collective work, organization, government, resistance, and collective ownership of the modes of production.

Well, now we are going to tell you what we want to do in the world and in Mexico. Because we cannot witness everything happening on our planet and remain quiet, as if we lived in a bubble.

Because what we want is to say to everyone who resists and struggles in some way in their countries, that they are not alone; that we, the Zapatistas, even though very small, support them and are going to look for a way to help them in their struggles and to dialogue with you to learn more, because the one thing we have learned is to study...

And we want to tell the world that we want to empower it, to the point where all those who resist will come together. Because the neoliberals want to destroy them for not allowing themselves to be pushed around. Instead, they fight for all of humanity.

In Mexico, what we want is to forge agreements with core leftists and organizations— because we think that it is on the political Left where one finds the idea of resisting neoliberal globalization—and to establish a country where there is justice, democracy, and freedom for all. It's not only recently that there is only justice for the rich, freedom for their immense businesses, and democracy if only to paint the fences with electoral propaganda. We think that a plan of struggle to save our country, Mexico, can only come from the Left.

And so with these leftists and organizations, we'll make a plan to go throughout Mexico where there are humble and simple people like ourselves. And it is not our place to go and tell them what to do or to order them around. Nor will we ask them to vote for a candidate, since we already know that the existing candidates are neoliberal. We are also not going to ask them to do what we do, or take up arms. What we will do is ask them about their lives, their struggles, the thought process of simple, humble people, and perhaps find in them the same love that we feel for our country.

And perhaps we will reach an agreement with them and together organize ourselves throughout the whole country and synchronize our struggles as right now they are isolated from one another, and find in the process a program that incorporates what we all want and a plan for how we are going to accomplish this National Program of Struggle.

We will find common ground with the majority as we build a universal struggle, with indigenous peoples, workers, peasants, students, teachers, women, children, men, and with all who have goodness in their hearts and the desire to fight so that our land— this place we call Mexico between the Río Grande and the Suchiate River, with the Pacific Ocean on one side and the Atlantic on the other—is not completely sold off and destroyed, (Sixth Declaration of the Lacandona Jungle, 2005: 244-247).

The elements of the Sixth Declaration of the Lacandona Jungle synthesize the proposal of the EZLN and allows us to identify actions relating to the construction of a world where we all have a place; in other words, the construction of another economy illuminates the path towards transforming relationships of injustice and oppression.

The fundamental element of the political solidarity economy is the construction of an economic alternative to the situation of poverty and marginalization through individual practices and self-organization. It is a long and enduring path. Within this same conception of the solidarity economy is expansiveness, the recognition of different processes and actors, different dimensions, and the need to advance towards the consolidation of solidarity networks, regional, national and international relationships; that is, to be present in the strategy to recover resources for all and create the conditions for a dignified life.

There is a very strong relationship between political solidarity economy, the processes of constructing autonomy for the people, the struggles of resistance, acts of solidarity, the struggle for peoples' rights, freedom, democracy, independence, the recognition of the rights of women and Indigenous people, self-determination, and freedom of choice. It is about an economic, political, social, and cultural struggle.

How Practices Become Strategic Actions

The political solidarity economy is an alternative model, a process that occurs in different places because of the need for people to turn into subjects or act in accordance with a decolonial, anti-system vision. In this way, it is a process that cannot be understood through integral, social, cultural, economic, and political practice. Within said practice, the elements that constitute a strategic action are acquired.

The transformation of practices into strategic actions happens through a long term process. When an activity is taken on in response to need, an explanation of the root cause is needed for problems such as food insecurity. The initial actions are concerned with the process of production, land, seeds, tools, input, water, the fertility of the land, and work. Within this first level, we understand the need for the organization of work, since collective organized action can help obtain a plan for production and adequate use of resources—this implies the systematization of the process of production, the administration of resources and time, knowledge of the costs of production and the mechanisms of distribution of the production and its benefits. This is what has happened among the different production collectives, as they have slowly looked at the possibility of creating alternatives to the experience of exploitation.

The collectives originate from a choice. They are sustained via communication, learning from all that is necessary to maintain a collective action, collective participation, constructing the path together, learning to maintain itself as a collective, resolving issues and finding solutions to issues of property and the equitable distribution of income, leadership, and shared responsibility.

The following step has to do with the structural issues of agricultural production, since there is an existing model that dominates via technology and market interests, i.e. conflicts over the control of prices and production, the role of peasants in the neoliberal model, the dispute over ownership of the modes of production, and the distribution of land.

The next level corresponds to the need to organize peasants and producers to defend their rights against the system of market control and the need to gain power as organized producers.

Because of this, after years of trying to have a place in the market and even with the practice of establishing fair trade markets in solidarity and as an alternative, the idea that it is necessary to look for an alternative path to the neoliberal model has been reached, which assumes the creation of a model with a different vision for resources, property, and the distribution of goods. Said vision understands the need for a more global transformation and emphasizes the construction of resources for the defense of territory and biodiversity; and at the same time, works with an idea of a future society and the need to develop resources to recover land, respect nature, and work to establish healthy relationships between people and nature. All of this makes possible the practice of freedom and reveals possibilities, i.e. that which corresponds to knowledge, hidden knowledge in ancestral practices, and what correlates with resistance. Accordingly, the initial action turns into a strategic action.

Therefore, food is not only produced but also comes with an awareness; furthermore, organization is strengthened, the people are bound together, a social force is constructed, and knowledge is produced for the future. Therein lies the wealth of a strategic action.

Spaces of Transformative Power

There are different spaces where transformative power can be observed, one of which is found in autonomous education. The first proposal of autonomous education responds to the need for education due to the mostly inefficient educational institutions in this country. This issue goes deeper because it turns into a collective action, since educators are part of the community.

The vision of this type of education is produced through vital life lessons, meaningful work, and solidarity. It is also produced through an understanding of current events, scientific knowledge, wisdom, and creativity. Moreover, it is a dialogue-based education that incorporates the accumulated wisdom of the community and includes resources for the future, a base to govern, pathways for the liberation of other peoples, a place in society with an autonomous education, participation and responsibility, and moving beyond oppression and erasure. Therefore, we aspire to an education that corresponds to knowledge acquired through praxis and knowledge that transform the mechanisms of domination.

With respect to the example of governing, it is about taking over the role of government and responding to community needs, listening, looking for ways to reach consensus, seeking justice, understanding plurality, learning the language of difference, establishing relationships with others, creating spaces for dialogue and communication, valuing dialogue and advice, having references for the actions of others, taking on responsibility, and working for the benefit of others.

These efforts can also be understood through the organized work of production and commodification via cooperatives that have their own bylaws, norms, and procedures; i.e. with mechanisms to make decisions, administrative capacity, direction, and a work plan. We speak of a process of formation in every sense, but in particular, to implement plans for global production and commodification with the knowledge of technology, media, and various tools.

The practice of collectives of production have a long history in Chiapas. Since the 1970s, the idea of collective work has been present and has always been related to community action. The decision to carry out collective work is made by people freely as a response to their needs, with the intention of strengthening their action and as an organizational practice and a space of learning which could activate the existing resources.

Throughout the long history of collective work, we find a diversity of organizational forms: from collectives that seek only to acquire resources to support community needs to those who resolve issues of malnutrition, health, and transportation—and in addition to service, production, and commercial cooperatives. In each case, there are ways of distributing goods, responsibility, and the organization of work.

In their own right, collectives emerge as a point of departure for various interests to practice cooperation, see the other, motivate action, experience the potential of the collective self, overcome fear and isolation, learn to act in an organized manner, become more aware of unity, relationships, direction, and wisdom. Collectives discover the demands of personal change in relation to equity, the universal recognition of rights, historical analysis, and the overcoming of mechanisms of marginalization and discrimination. Communities are constructed from their own reality when they are able to look beyond their own interests and survive the perils of capitalist development; in this way, they gain a vision of another world.

The most complex example of the organizational process of communities is the production and commercialization of coffee. On the one hand, this product can be produced through an organized collective using agro-ecological practices; i.e. from an understanding of the need to produce coffee without neglecting to produce basic foods, learning to manage the coffee farm with proper tools during the process of production and harvesting. On the other hand, there is the organizing process to go to market in the alternative solidarity market, which implies consolidating relationships through a fair solidarity market, while establishing commercial relationships through the legal frameworks for exportation and importation using international currency—in addition to whatever else is implied by marketing, toasting, milling, bottling, and branding in another country.

This process is built to reinforce the bonds of solidarity and show a path toward another economy. The construction of alternatives for the global situation at the local level is a very delicate process in the sense that an action to construct alternatives to the capitalist model can be overwhelmed by capitalist interests.

8.2 What are the Features of this Alternative World

ORGANIZING IS THE EASIEST ASPECT TO UNDERSTAND. It derives from the community itself, born of its own volition, produced through the individual participation of everyone, and constructed through experience and practice. This becomes knowledge sustained and fortified through social collective practice. It also develops a vision of reality and confronts it, understands the historical and structural situation, takes into account the material situation of all, and understands itself to be a process in which we grow despite our personal limitations.

Another alternative model is the knowledge of freedom through practice; this is the knowledge to be free, the phenomenon of ideas, which corresponds to the processes of reflection, analysis, and life experience. There is also scaling upwards, in the sense that there is an effort to establish relationships that are increasingly expansive, taking into account geography and plurality, while making sense of an expansive global plurality, an alternative society, and learning to be guided by the paths of many.

The added benefits correspond to the distribution of goods, the defense and creation of territory, nutrition, health, education and capacity building through the power of community, organization, well being, energy, and hope.

Strengthening the local economy within the context of a wider economy acts on the principle that no one gets stronger if they do not operate within an expansive context, which provides the only opportunity to construct alternatives to capitalism. The need for a change in the broad sense, including that which determines local events, is the foundation of strengthening local economies. This is to acknowledge that the conservation of forests, water sources, and the defense of life and territory depend on a change in the global structure, and so our universal commitment is to life. Therefore, it is not about profit in the hands of the few, but rather equitable distribution of goods and the exercise of universal participation.

Primary Goals and Obstacles

The primary goals refer in particular to the need to construct the alternative. There is a constant organized practice of production and commercialization, which takes into account agroecology. The most important are commercial cooperatives, artisanal crafts, and coffee. This achievement is due to many years of labor, advocacy, communication, and study, as well as the understanding of the importance of territory, biodiversity, strategic resources, and the need to construct through one's individual effort, while connecting with local, regional, national and international experiences.

In this way, it becomes possible to overcome the limitations of not having received a formal education or a specialized capacity for certain types of labor. Therefore, having food, resources for health care, being organized, being part of an organization that respects everyone's rights, seeking to have parity from a gender standpoint, and establishing collaborative relationships with different peoples, may be seen as important achievements.

Merit consists in identifying ourselves as subjects who are capable of collective action, who own resources, who are organized, and who have the knowledge and strength to resist. In autonomous communities, work and practices that transform relationships are visible, such as the equitable distribution of land, fair and respectful relationships between communities—which, despite conflict and harassment, make consensus and peace possible—maintain open dialogue, avoid falling into counterinsurgent provocations, and have hope.

The limitations are structural, which is why it is necessary to grow and achieve meaningful results in the production of food, soil recovery, and the expansion of collectives—without losing sight that this is about collective action.

What is a Future Action?

Constructing the future is an alternative to the system of domination. We are constructing a future built on freedom, where you can see women's strength as they have their say, make their decisions, and share their wisdom. It is the future of nature, the consolidation of bonds of solidarity, the exchange of goods and knowledge, the opening of spaces of participation, daring to imagine an alternative to the reality of marginalization, working with others, listening, seeing, caring and making proposals. It is about working at the local level to transform unjust relationships of domination through solidarity practices.

Chapter Nine

Reflection on the Radical Nature of Political Solidarity Economy

WE ARE FACED WITH BROAD RELATIONSHIPS THAT CAN DICTATE LOCAL, INDIVIDUAL, AND SOCIAL ACTION AND PROVIDE THE OPPORTUNITY FOR A CHANGE in the relationships of submission and exploitation. These changes may imply the construction of irreversible alternatives. Likewise, there may be a return and spiral path, but we will have learned something along the way at each turn. Therefore, each step will be a collective learning experience that will allow us to move forward.

Also, there is the possibility down the road of overcoming the challenges of our current context. In the same way, there are visions that can help us understand this process: collective action, a sense of adventure, and daring to realize dreams of freedom.

There is historical injustice against women. The situation of women is part of the fight for the rights of the communities. We need to practice the right to speak, think, and work in an organized manner, and participate in building a just society. Women must join together in the goal of ending their suffering; they must learn what it takes to go out and be free. Therefore, we recognize the capacity of women to work, lead, and participate. The tasks for men include to not impede the rights of women, to offer knowledge and experience to support them; and to reinvent themselves as men who share housework, childcare and production. However, to achieve this type of equality, we must work consistently. It won't get done overnight. We also need to understand and appreciate the value of women's thinking and work in the world.

Over time, various experiences have emerged that can help illustrate how political solidarity economy takes shape. These are astonishingly radical actions, in contrast to actions that reaffirm situations of marginalization, enslavement, and hopelessness. Here are some steps that allow us to identify specific aspects of the solidarity economy:

The New Path

Out of necessity, hope is born. The new path is born in the very heart of the community as a break from the past in which there are no more injustices, sorrows, or sadness.

We are going to build a refuge for all as a rebuke of the master's house. This is a new and righteous path, which has cultural significance, historical weight, and is rooted in identity. It is based on the responsibility of historical subjects who make a new world and a new society possible.

It fills us with joy to recognize that this path constitutes the hope of communities. It is the path that different organizations travel; it is an open, grand, and beautiful road, which is manifested in the construction of autonomy.

If we see into the heart of the communities, we will find the desire for autonomy as a response to a situation of dependency and humiliation; it is a cry and a hope.

The Root and Resistance

The need for one's own path is present in the people's resistance to domination and neglect. When we meditate on the chains that bind us to lies and deception, we realize that deep within us there is dignity.

One of the great actions that the communities have undertaken has been the recovery of historical memory; that is, the realization that they belong to the past and that they are the product of a historical process. At the same time, they have discovered the great power they have to fight for dignity, respect for people, and collective decisions. The importance of resistance is the recognition of one's own strengths and abilities, and sharpening them accordingly.

Resistance is also a new path traveled by previous generations. The ancestors gave us examples of resistance, they taught us to recognize our roots and showed us that if we eat from the roots we will survive and bear fruit. If we hold tight to this story, we will generate hope. This vision starts from the prophetic word that we learned. At our root is the past of great civilizations; in the words of the Father, who recognizes us in freedom, it is our vocation.

Bread and Nourishment

We want everyone to eat, to avoid hunger, to learn to recognize the suffering of others, to know that from our work it is possible to have food, because everyone's work helps us survive.

Organizing communities makes it possible for alternatives, knowledge, technologies, and new lessons to exist. The practice of collective work makes it possible for bread to be distributed among all. Common work is the ideal place to learn, develop, and practice virtues and values; it is an invitation to participate and share the joy of the harvest.

The Seed

The seeds have been sown for a new society with freedom, justice, and new relationships. The seed for new life is the effort of many generations, which is why it takes time, since now is just the time for planting seeds.

The fields and new approaches have opened, we see them blooming in celebration of hope; we have gathered these seeds through pain and with hope—they are the fruit of the work. When we meet to discuss our needs, learn, review our work, plan actions, and listen to our hearts, we are sowing hope.

The Source

We have discovered an unlimited fountain from which to drink: the commitment that uplifts us, the dialogue that transforms us, the truth that guides us. Therefore, we are bound by the truth of freedom. The source is born from our needs and the reality of what we are and have. From the depths of our being, the strength to work hard is born—it is a cry.

Childbirth

It is the joy of seeing the emergence of consciousness, the way new relationships are established, the steps of those who learn to walk through their own effort, pain and joy, the way they speak and dialogue, the new spark in their gaze; the spirit of one who creates the alternatives, the sense of belonging; the heart; the rupture of routine, dependence, domination and the path to eternity; as well as the way in which the community celebrates this creative capacity, pain notwithstanding, since the new being is free.

The Horizon

We walk towards the future. What we do makes sense, since we hope that our daughters and sons will have a better future. We recognize the dawn of a new day and we are motivated to reach the horizon. It is now time to plant seeds. Our hopes lie in the future, let's not lose heart.

We discovered the need for a complete future and horizon, as well as a true and familiar promise—this is the legacy to which we are entitled. We are headed back home. We have broken the chains that held us in place and left us without hope. Our eyes see where we will end up.

Hands

We build everything through our work, commitment, responsibility, and conviction. The work is expressed by experienced hands working together. Through taking action, we have hope, and through work, we awaken. We awake thinking about what we represent, since we are characters who belong in this story because of our work. Our momentum grows through our participation because this work is ours, it has our color and countenance. Therefore, no one is left out—we are all necessary.

Better Skies Over The New Earth

We recognize that our work shapes new skies over the new promised land, since it is a path of justice based on mutual support, solidarity, with roots in identity and the law, establishing itself through language and dialogue because of its demands. .

Dedicating one's life to the people, sharing food, working together with respect and trust, recognizing the needs of others, refusing to give up despite obstacles, walking even when feeling weary, and the joy of discovering new paths are the signs of this new heaven and earth.

9.1 Strategic Objectives

POLITICAL SOLIDARITY ECONOMY CAN HELP US TO CARRY OUT THIS EFFORT OVER TIME, since it is man-made, evocative, like a guide to align one's own experience with this strategy, just as in large stadiums in which work and the structures that constitute the space are raised simultaneously. In this example, space is important—the structures only serve to support the space.

This great strategic construction must guide all actions taken. In this sense, this book seeks to outline the stages we must undergo for the political solidarity economy to become a true alternative.

It is easy to grasp the vision of constructing the political solidarity economy. This happens when we consider only one aspect of the economy such as the collective production of goods or community organization. It is necessary to have a global structure in which all actions, processes, and elements acquire meaning in order to make possible the transformation of relationships.

There is a passion that drives these anarchist acts. However, by having a strategic understanding, the possibility arises of seeing the role that each transformative action and subject plays.

The Social Subjects

Constructing a space with relationships is made possible through the emergence of civil society. We're talking about a social construction that can only happen through transformative actions. The fundamental objective of a transformative action must be the construction of the social subject who will confront reality—to the extent they develop as a subject, since this is where the ability to accept other challenges is found. The construction of the subject is one of the elements that accompanies collective action.

Collective action requires a structure that must agree on a plan of action. Within the exchange of goods, for example, it is important to create a structure that takes into account the processes and costs of production, transportation, and the time necessary for this work, so that when establishing the mechanisms of exchange, equitable relationships can be established. In addition, spaces and services, amounts, population, needs, calendar, climate, vehicles, circulation of goods and people, etc. must be anticipated from an organizational perspective. The construction of these structures is increasingly complex, since it allows the collective subject to acquire the ability to do what is necessary while moving towards broader and more meaningful actions.

The beginning depends on each group and their developed capacity, with the intention of moving towards more comprehensive actions in which systemic conditions that do not allow fair relationships to be established can be taken into account. For this reason, the economy is prioritized as the place for constructing subjects. It is they who face the reality of exploitation and competition in the market within the economy—taking into account how market competition is the war for the profit and dispossession of existing resources such as staple foods, which are increasingly limited given their fundamental role in providing subsistence.

The defense of the land against transnational interests is fundamental. To establish such protection, organizing the population on an inclusive and profound level is essential. Furthermore, it is necessary to have knowledge of the land's resources and an action strategy to resist the onslaught that comes from the interests of the neoliberal model at the national and international level.

In this way, the structure of collective production and the commercialization and exchange of basic goods are not enough. A more complex organization with political capacity is needed in order to create alternatives to the neoliberal model in relation to existing resources. It would be necessary to propose a production model based on the use of resources, with the intention of permanently maintaining resources permanently, without depleting the land, water, and biodiversity.

In practice, the solidarity political economy must incorporate organizational capacity, a breadth of knowledge, and the tools to achieve different results without reproducing the same conditions that one wants to change. It is an impassioned exercise. Given how the production process is made possible with all necessary elements, individuals capable of transforming unjust relationships in that same space are created. Therefore, they are not two separate acts—the subject who performs the work also helps to transform relationships.

To achieve this goal, it is important to always strive for it. Accordingly, the methodology of collective action will give rise to social subjects. Thus, there are elements such as raised consciousness; the ability to experience, feel, and speak out in the face of reality that corresponds to the appropriation of the subject, which, in turn, implies the capacity for indignation, the desire to contribute to the construction of a just society, and political commitment.

For its part, collective action—with its ties to the processes of production, exchange, and distribution of goods—has other dimensions. In addition, it is a space to grow with respect to the knowledge of the broader society, the mechanisms of power, development strategies, solutions to global challenges regarding the depletion and misappropriation of resources. Ultimately, it is about the transformation of unjust relationships and the mechanisms of unequal appropriation of goods

Economic Theory

There can be no economic theory without praxes and the historical need for transformation. While we have promoted the practice of the political solidarity economy, an effort has arisen to have a theoretical framework of it, with an analysis of poverty and marginalization, development models, the dominant system of production, and capitalism.

This effort is part of the meetings and documents put together to find solutions to this reality. Without this elaboration of proposals and analysis, the relations of exploitation, dispossession, accumulation, and deterioration of the existing model could not have been transformed. Beyond utopias, we have achieved a serious analysis of the alternatives to the neoliberal model, with consideration for the historical practice of socialism with all its contributions and interpretations regarding the transformation of the social relations of production.

It is very important to realize that we understand the political solidarity economy not as a public policy of self-appointed democratic governments or as the construction of State socialism, but rather, as an anti-systemic practice led by workers, organized Indigenous communities, as the processes of organized civil society against ties of oppression, subjugation, and dispossession and in favor of new connections to justice and well-being.

This search has led us to understand the superior values of the political solidarity economy: horizontal power structure, trade, the production of goods and services, collective property, collective work, solidarity, and the exercise of self-determination. That is, a set of elements that have led us, rightly so, to the comparison of the different models.

Therefore, what we present is not the theoretical basis of the political solidarity economy, but a theoretical conception whose development is ongoing. We have approached the reality in which we live, the concrete conditions with all their limitations and potentialities, understanding that the current situation is the synthesis of multiple factors and the product of a set of social, political, economic and structural bonds. We know that if we delve into this reality, we will find a reflection of the global system, i.e. what we have done with the production of corn and coffee, the situation of women, the deterioration of nature, the depletion of resources, etc. Despite this, the ways to transform colonial oppression arise from this approach to reality.

When Marx set about the task of deciphering the essence of capitalism, as a historical system determined by social production, he did not, at any point, start down the path of inductive reasoning of all the instances of capitalist development that exist upon the earth during his time, with no exceptions whatsoever. As a dialectician, he has proceeded otherwise; he took the most characteristic and the most developed case, namely, the English capitalist and mercantile reality, and developed a universal economic theory based mainly on a detailed study of this unique case.

This study was based on the notion that the universal laws of capitalist development are the same for all countries and that England, the country that went furthest down the path of capitalist development, epitomized the purest expression of the capitalist system.

What exists in other countries is a state of inferior and obscure imitation, or as a trend yet to fully manifest, or that is defined and complicated by accompanying external circumstances, was entirely developed in England in the purest classical form. Marx did not rely on certain features of capitalist development in other countries except in certain well-defined cases (for example, he referred to numerous aspects of economic development in the Russian countryside for an analysis on wages) (Vasílievich, 1975: 58).

We do not have to look far to find traits of capitalist ways of production in the Chiapas countryside or the interests of the transnationals regarding the strategic resources necessary for the global machinery. To explain the construction of the alternatives, we adopted a strategy that honed in on the differences between the neoliberal economy and the solidarity economy, seeing as how the economy is a universal law of work based on the production of goods and services with the same resources—thus, a shared temporal and spatial relationship for everyone.

The strategy that we will present below served to advance and discover new possibilities for the construction of current conditions against subjugation.

Table graph

Indicators	Neoliberal Economy	Solidarity Economy
1. The role of work	Productivity	a) Satisfy needs b) Realize yourself as a person
2. The organization of work	In hierarchical form, the owners are the bosses	a) Democratic b) Contribute to the whole c) Make decisions in the assembly d) As culture
3. Technology	Substitution of human labor	a) An instrument of work
4. The land	a) Merchandise b) Individual property c) Enterprise	a) Sustenance b) Collective or individual property for collective use
5. Production	For the market	a) Auto-consumption b) Exchange c) Market

6. The price of products	Depends on offer and demand	According to work and in relationship to other products
7. The market	Controlled by the great companies and the global banks	Controlled by producers and consumers depending on their real needs
8. Money	Merchandise, power	Mode of exchange
9. Relationships	Domination	Cooperation and the construction of power
10. Space	Competition	Free

Although it is not the subject of this book, the study of economic theory and its history is necessary. In any case, you should take note of the historical path of constructing alternatives to understand the process of constructing the economy and the relationships of production. In the 1970s, DESMI had the opportunity to systematize some concepts by making a dictionary of initial definitions by starting a qualitative analysis, and most were related to the economy. According to this dictionary:

In the process of production, exchange, distribution and consumption of material goods, economic relations are established between people—regardless of their consent and their will. The relations of production are a necessary part of any mode of production. Social production can only occur when people come together to work together to establish an exchange of activities. The basis of production is found in the relationship of ownership over the means of production.

The character of relationships of production depends on who owns the means of production and on how the union of these means with the producers is realized.

History knows two fundamental types of property: private and communal. Private property expresses relations of dominance and subordination, since the owners of the means of production have the possibility of exploiting those without property. Throughout its upward trajectory, the relations of production based on the exploitation of labor appear under enslaving, feudal, and capitalist forms. Social property eliminates exploitative relationships, gives rise to collaboration. Under the regime of a primitive community, it existed in the form of collective gentile and tribal property. Presently, the socialist relations of production are based on two forms of property: the state (of all the people) and the cooperative.

In the 1970s, we did not yet understand political solidarity economy. This process was constructed through the 80s and continued until the 90s. Hence, we now have a clear and complete understanding of the subject.

José Luis Coraggio underscored the urgency to build and institutionalize an economy where everyone has a place, a self-sustaining economy, and an economy of solidarity that provides a material response to the legitimate desires of all citizens (2008):

That is why the Other Economy, whether we propose it discursively or through our practices, must be social, because it must not only produce and distribute material goods and services but also generate and enable other social relationships, other relationships with nature, other modes of reproduction, and alternative living conditions in society unlike the model of possessive individualist capitalism. As a consequence, we wouldn't have economic growth measured by the annual Gross Domestic Product as a development indicator, nor would we assume that more is better (overproduction). Because the famous spillover of art into the market has shown itself to actually be a process of concentrating wealth in the hands of a few, as a means for exploitation, or simply the exclusion of workers. And because capitalist and state-socialist industrial growth has shown that its immediate logic of abundance has led to crossing boundaries that generate potentially irreversible ecological imbalances.

Learning cannot ignore the theoretical formation of the great anarchist movements, such as Paulo Freire's Pedagogy of the Oppressed, national liberation movements, liberation theology, and the revolutions of Cuba, Chile, Nicaragua, Guatemala, El Salvador and all of insurgent America. In addition, we learn from the resistance and rebellion of native peoples, whose ancestral wisdom gives us a primordial relationship with Mother Earth and with ourselves.

I want to end this reflection on economic theory by quoting part of the Insurgent Subcomandante Marcos's thoughts to clarify the meaning of the theoretical creation that accompanies transformative processes.

Fourteen years ago, with the October moon hovering over path, in the southeast mountains of Mexico, the last details of the uprising were being fine-tuned. I say "fine-tuning the last details" just to repeat a common phrase. In reality, we walked from one place to another, with much ease to ponder the possible political and military success of an armed uprising of thousands of Indigenous people and the seizure of seven municipal seats in the southeastern Mexican state of Chiapas.

Making the final preparations for the uprising resembled the effort of carving with a hammer and chisel one of those tiny diamond jewels that amaze for their colors and brilliance. So it was then and still is today.

Our cause—the freedom for Indigenous communities—the most beautiful, noble, and ancient in the history of humanity; has so many tones and hues that, even now, on the brink of 24 years of committing ourselves to it, we've yet to fully grasp it (Insurgent Subcomandante Marcos, 2008: 4).

9.2 Concrete Application and Collective Practice

THE CONCRETE IMPLEMENTATION AND COLLECTIVE PRACTICE of the political solidarity economy are central aspects for the transformation of reality. This transformation is like sculpting a figure from a block of marble. In other words, it is a transformation that is the result of a set of consistent actions.

DESMI proposed a way to practice this collective work through ten principles:

1. Membership and Voluntary Withdrawal

It is the will of each member to participate in the work group, committing to the interests and needs of the entire group or to withdraw, if they so wish.

2. Voting

Everyone who participates in the group must remain committed, build consensus for decision-making, and attend group meetings and assemblies.

3. Comprehensive Training

The members of the collective or cooperative can and should be trained in everything necessary to improve collective work.

4. Rules

Regulations are a series of internal laws that correspond to collective or cooperative work. They can only be arranged and agreed upon by the partners who will follow them.

5. Mutual Support

The collective or cooperative will learn from other groups and share work experience, maintaining communication with them by holding meetings and visits to help and strengthen themselves.

6. Work with Nature

Collective work will help all of us to have a better life, protecting and strengthening nature, i.e. Mother Earth, and everything that inhabits her: people, plants, animals, water, and minerals.

7. Respect for Differences

In a collective or cooperative the most important thing is to have common goals, accountability, and rules. Political, religious or ethnic differences will be respected and considered as the cultural wealth of the group.

8. Discretion

Discretion can be the group's "best friend." Outside of work meetings or around strangers, you should avoid talking about the internal affairs of the group.

9. Work on Behalf of the Community

Collective work must always be linked to community-wide improvement, open to working with new partners, and respectful towards the work and projects of other people or groups.

10. Clear and Efficient Administration

Making plans, organizing work, coordinating and managing everyone's tasks, as well as maintaining control over all group activities to make possible a clear and efficient administration that is fundamental for an environment of trust and security within collective work.

In DESMI's brochure "Collective Work, Cooperative Work," the following principles were elaborated with the practice and tradition of cooperative work. In this way, they teach us that the process starts from below. And so it is a constant practice that allows us to build, in a solid way, the necessary alternatives and overcome our limitations. Without this practice, the strength of a real and concrete proposal would be illegitimate.

For this reason, it is important to consider the great diversity of social and organizational practices that exist in the world; to open the universe of uplifting movements, since is innumerable knowledge, learning and reflections of reality, the conditions of marginalization, oppression and forgetfulness. It is important to become aware of the existence of these practices, learn to approach them, discover their strengths, understand what is produced, perceive the elements of the alternative model of society that is born from this creativity in constant production.

We need to use all available means, initiatives, visits, electronic media, internet, meetings, forums. Above all, we need to have a detailed and meticulous analysis of what is happening within each specific practice and without detaching it from its history and context. All these practices occupy a real, concrete space and constitute, in some way, the defense of the land by civil society.

The fact is that these concrete practices exist, and they are part of the powerful energy that makes life possible at all levels. One of the necessary tasks is the sharing of experiences at the local, regional, national and international levels, in which the relationships that build networks under territorial occupation are established.

Faced with the debacle caused by careless consumption of strategic resources, there are concrete, ethical actions—with a vision of the future—which will ultimately show that another world, other relationships, and other interests are possible.

It will take time for us to understand that the Zapatistas have invited collective action from below, utilizing a long and profound history within a great diversity of circumstances.

The Zapatistas produced a series of textbooks:

Freedom According to the Zapatistas, Autonomous Government I, Autonomous Government II, Autonomous Resistance, Participation of Women in Autonomous Government.

From the last text, *Participation of women in autonomous government* (2014), I will quote some paragraphs in which the meaning of building from below is articulated.

1. *Within the work that we have been doing, as time went by, we encountered difficulties that prevented us from doing work for the struggle. In some towns there wasn't or there isn't moral support that some or many of us need as women who are either participating or taking a stand, and more so if we feel unable to perform the work that we have to do. Another difficulty is perhaps the fear of making mistakes in the jobs that we have to perform, or the fear that colleagues will make fun of our involvement, despite everyone working their way up from the same source.*

2. *That perhaps there wasn't enough courage to face or solve a problem, even if it is the smallest thing that takes place in the course of our work for the struggle. Perhaps because there wasn't a certain will or the effort to develop our capacity as women.*

3. *Having many children also caused us women not to dedicate more time to our corresponding jobs in the Zapatista struggle. This difficulty became greater when the compañero in the family did not take on the responsibility of caring for and supporting the children when the compañera went to work.*

4. *The fourth challenge that we find as compañeras and that we have often faced is the problem of education, not knowing how to read and write. Maybe it's because we didn't have anyone to teach us, especially the compañeras who were already grown up in 1994, when it started. Sometimes a colleague is given a position and the first thing she tells us is "I don't know how to read or write." Perhaps she is right, because before '94, there was no education for our parents (9-10).*

9.3 Continental References in this Practice

AN INTERVIEW WITH INMANUEL WALLERSTEIN, conducted by Antoine Reverchon (2008), demonstrates the magnitude of constructing an alternative to capitalism with a vision of the future and with all the energy and power of critical and creative humanity.

Capitalism is omnivorous, it captures profit where it matters most at any given moment. Not content with modest fringe benefits, on the contrary, it maximizes them by building monopolies. Lately, it has tried to do so once again through biotechnologies and information technologies. But I think that the possibilities of real accumulation by the system has reached its limit. Capitalism, since its birth in the second half of the sixteenth century, has been fed by the difference in wealth between a center in which profits converge, as well as increasingly impoverished (not necessarily geographical) peripheries.[7]

We are in a rather strange period in which the crisis and the impotence of the powerful leave room for universal free will: today, there is a period during which each of us has the possibility to influence the future through our individual action. But since that future will be the sum of an incalculable amount of those actions, it is absolutely impossible to foresee which model will end up prevailing. In ten years, perhaps it will become clearer; in thirty or forty years, a new system will have emerged. I think, unfortunately, it is just as possible that we see the installation of a system of exploitation even more violent than capitalism, rather than the establishing of a more egalitarian and redistributive model.

The interests of neoliberalism define the situation of dispossession and deterioration in Chiapas. Violence and war are part of this strategy. At the same time, we can see an energy

---

[7]   Wallerstein, Immanuel. Interview by Antoine Reverchon. El Capitalismo Acaba, 18 Nov. 2008. https://rebelion.org/el-capitalismo-se-acaba/

crisis, the destruction of nature, and ongoing resource depletion. This dynamic is made worse because these interests do not want to allow wealth in the hands of the indigenous people and leave us outside the system. In this way, it seems that there is no future or meaning to life, that there is no other way out.

Looking in a different direction, we will find ways of construction within communities, an ancient awareness of respect for nature, cooperation, and a sense of the future. Building from below is the alternative with multiple strategies in an open space, as well as the search for solutions to poverty and marginalization in a just society.

A solidarity political economy cannot be built without transnational references, since the different methods of work and distribution produce an alternative to neoliberalism. For this reason, a global vision is necessary, with which it can be said that these processes exist everywhere.

Global Vision and Political Solidarity Economy

Below are some economic practices linked to the solidarity political economy:

→   Worker-led management of companies
→   Solidarity fair trade
→   Branded organizations
→   Ecological agriculture
→   Conscious consumption
→   Solidarity consumption
→   Local Employment and Trade Systems (LETS).
→   Social Barter Systems (SEL).
→   Community Exchange Systems (SEC).
→   The global barter network
→   The economy of communion
→   Micro-loans and reciprocal credit systems
→   Community banks
→   Ethical banking
→   Solidarity shopping groups

→ Boycott movements
→ Local systems of social currencies
→ The dissemination of open source software

The following will present the general information that motivated the construction of the solidarity political economy:

A. Statistics show that at the end of the millennium there were 6.1 billion inhabitants in the world. Most people in the world live in poverty, but with the power to create an alternative system. This reality reminds us of the importance of an ethnic map of Latin America. At the First Earth Summit, in Rio de Janeiro (1992), an observation was made regarding the major problems affecting survival, which led to a commitment to reverse the imbalance between man and nature.

B. Technological development in productive, social, and cultural life goes hand in hand with the information revolution and technological communication. Globalization would not have been possible otherwise.

C. The constitution of the Intercontinental Network of Social Solidarity Economy (RIPESS). The main objective was to establish national, regional and international links with actors of the solidarity economy to achieve the strengthening of its global impact (www.ripess. net).

D. The First Gathering on the Globalization of Solidarity in Lima, Peru (1997) allowed various networks and activists of the Social and Solidarity Economy (ESS) worldwide to exchange their experiences and practices in this field. Thus, the social and solidarity economy was defined as the set of economic activities and practices with a social purpose that contributes to the construction of a new way of thinking and living the economy. Social entrepreneurship is different because of its impact on local development and the effort to impact communities, mainly through job creation, offering new services, improvements to quality of life, ecological preservation, and ethical conditions for the creation of wealth.

E. The First Continental Gathering and the First Intercontinental Gathering for Humanity and Against Neoliberalism were convened by the EZLN in April and June of 1996.

F. An important group of organizations and movements spoke out against globalization that sought to impose itself globally through the World Trade Organization. In response, alternative proposals for another global economic model were presented in Seattle, United States in 1999 and in Davos, Switzerland in 2000.

G. The First World Social Forum in Papua, Italy in April 2000, which promoted economic and political democracy. The Liliput Network declared: "We must be able to build a network that knows how to unite, link, and strengthen people and initiatives that seek to weave the threads of a regulated economy according to social justice and environmental respect [...]; A network of networks is needed that knows how to combine efforts towards a truly sustainable and equitable economy, which will be able to stop all the consequences of economic globalization (Launch of La Rete de Liliput: alleanze, obiettivi, strategie, Bologna, EMI , 2001).

World social forums became important spaces for the empowerment of solidarity organizations, through the inter-network connections promoted by them. The motto of the meeting in Montreal, Canada (2000) was "resist and build." In addition, an International Liaison Committee (CIE, in its Spanish acronym) was created as an instrument for continuous dialogue between the different continents, but also to promote resistance to neoliberalist strategies and build effective and lasting alternatives.

400 representatives of solidarity economy organizations from Europe, Latin America, North America, Africa, and Asia participated. The main development was the diffusion of a collective consensus in increasingly growing sectors regarding the fact that the solidarity economy can become an alternative to capitalism.

In this sense, special attention should be given to reflections on how to connect organizations in solidarity networks; reconstituting production chains; integrating financing, production, marketing and consumption processes; as well as seeking to achieve greater autonomy from capitalist organizations and material flows of economic value. The event held in Brazil in 2001 focused international attention on Porto Alegre and Rio Grande do Sul. The alternatives that were built in conjunction with those popular governments used for international reflection. Thus, there was not only reflection on how the society democratically appropriated political instruments in those places—as in the case of the participatory budget—but also on the possibility of an economically viable, socially just, and ecologically sustainable development, in which consumers and workers become the main economic agents, with the spread of a culture of solidarity that adds economic growth with income distribution. Participants represented 122 countries with 1,502 foreign delegates, 16 round tables and about 400 workshops, with an audience of approximately 20,000 people.

The Global Network for Solidarity Socioeconomics (RGSES, in its Spanish acronym) was launched at the World Social Forum in 2001. In the RGSES' press release, it was stated that the following criteria were considered the minimum for participation:

a)   No form of exploitation in the network's initiatives;

b)   That participants seek to preserve the ecological balance of ecosystems;

c)   That they are willing to share significant economic profits, rebuilding production chains in a solidarity and ecological way, generating jobs and distributing income to guarantee economic conditions for the exercise of public and individual freedoms based on an ethic of solidarity.

The Intercontinental Network of Social Solidarity Economy extended an invitation to share wealth, lessons learned, and the challenges identified within the field of the social and solidarity economy to deepen a collective formation, as well as the analysis and capacity to take action and try to give shape to an progressive vision and set priorities for the promotion of the solidarity economy worldwide.

The Fourth Assembly of the Peoples' UN, held in Perusia, Italy in October 2001, promoted the idea that network dynamics can advance in the construction of a post-capitalist society.

For its part, the Encounter in Dakar, Senegal, from October 22-26, 2005, was supported by various Canadian organizations such as *"Development and Peace,"* Quebec organizations involved in the solidarity economy, and the *Catholique contre la faim et pour le Développement* Committee

(CCFD, in its French acronym). The five themes around which the workshops were organized in Dakar were solidarity finance, popular alternatives to privatization, local development, ethical and solidarity trade, and the promotion of the social and solidarity economy.

In January 2006, the Sixth World Social Forum held three events in the cities of Bamako (Mali), Caracas (Venezuela) and Karachi (Pakistan). The solidarity economy represents one of the pressing themes of the CCFD, which arranges different spaces for reflection at the international level in world social forums—as well as in the French platform for fair trade—with the intention of supporting the participation of its counterparts and promoting contact and participation in networks.

It is also important to follow up on the forum on sustainability held in Hong Kong in 2011.

From January 25-27, 2013, the Summit of the Communities of Latin America, the Caribbean and Europe for Social Justice, International Solidarity and the Sovereignty of Indigenous People was held in Santiago de Chile. At this summit, every social, popular, and political movement in Chile was summoned to join and make their demands heard so the struggles and resistance to unjust policies would find a space for articulation and the construction of alternatives.

The intercontinental RIPESS proposed some activities related to the general purposes of the Intercontinental Forum of Social and Solidarity Economy in October 2013 in the Philippines: the construction of a global vision of the social and solidarity economy, tools for its interconnection and visualization, and public policies around the world. This global event was chaired by the world forums held in Lima, Quebec, Dakar and Luxembourg in 2009.

The Manila event, for its part, had as its main purpose the theme "Building the Social and Solidarity Economy as an Alternative Development Model." Similarly, networks and organizations around the world were invited to participate in the First World Forum of Social and Solidarity Economy of RIPESS in Asia.

Various organizations and people gathered at the National Meeting of the Social and Solidarity Economy, called "Solidarity is an Act of Peace," held in the city of Bogotá in 2013. They agreed to express themselves against the negotiations between the national government and the representatives of the Revolutionary Armed Forces of Colombia (FARC, in its Spanish acronym) to resolve the country's armed conflict.

In November 2013, the sixth edition of the bi-annual Conference of Leaders of the Social and Solidarity Economy was organized. About 350 people from 45 countries met in Chamonix, France to dialogue, share experiences, and develop projects. There, it was proposed, among other things, to become aware of the interdependence of the planet's inhabitants and articulate the value of the common good on a global scale—in addition to establishing collaboration for the production and fair access to these goods, prohibiting the appropriation and private management of common goods, and carrying out adequate governance. Alternatives were explored to replace the logic of competition and achieve social and environmental results, based on the business models of the ESS[8] which prioritize individual empowerment and growth. It was also proposed to create qualitative indicators of well-being to measure the income of the ODMS[9] after 2015.

Some proposed indicators were the creation of ESS companies, a) the number of jobs created and maintained, b) the stability of structures created c) the ecological footprint of various human activities d) citizen participation through the ESS in favor of responsible production and consumption and equal distribution of wealth e) structuring trade around three strategic axes: a change in the direction, scale, method and model of doing business.

Social movements and civil society organizations from different parts of the world met in September 2013 in Saint Petersburg, Russia, on the eve of the G-20 Summit, as the United States of America threatened to attack Syria. The summit was sponsored with the participation of more than 30 international delegates from the post-globalization initiative.

Likewise, the vision of peasants, fishermen, women, working men, communities, indigenous people, and the LGBTQIA+ community was expressed, as well as all the communities around the world who speak out in favor of changing the system.

---

8   Translator's note: Social Solidarity Economy
9   Translator's note: Original Design Manufacturers

However, G20 has not risen to this task, not even to reform, in a lasting way, world capitalism. Therefore, G20 is not legitimate, democratic or transparent. Five years after the financial crisis, G20 continues to promote failed neoliberal policies. The cooptation of so-called emerging economies like the BRICS in Brazil, Russia, India, China, and South Africa is not a departure from neoliberal globalization. On the contrary, these countries have also provided funds to the IMF, including $75 billion USD in 2012 to continue the imposition of austerity measures in countries facing a deep recession and social crisis.

We want a world in which the productive socialization of the world economy is achieved in a democratic way. The market, however, privatizes wealth and socializes poverty, repression, and ecological destruction. Therefore, we reaffirm the supremacy of human rights and democracy over markets and finances.

In Latin America, several organizations build alternative experiences of production, commercialization, and strengthen solidarity and popular economies, such as:

→ The CEDAC and the MST in Brazil

→ DESMI in Chiapas, Mexico

→ The National Association of Workers in Self-Governance and Stock Participation Companies (ANTEAG, in its Spanish acronym)

→ The Latin American Confederation of Cooperatives and Mutual Workers (COLACOT, in its Spanish acronym)

→ The International School of Culture and Solidarity Economy (ECOSOL, in its Spanish acronym)

→ The Promotion of Popular Development (PDP, in its Spanish acronym)

→ The Brazilian Network of Solidarity Socioeconomics, made up of companies and collaborators from the Brazilian Meeting of Solidarity Culture and Socioeconomics.

→ The group of women in savings, loans, and productive projects in southern Sonora since 1990. In the 2002 assembly, the president of the society defined the organization as *"an autonomous association of women from popular and peasant neighborhoods, which have voluntarily come together to meet common socio-economic and cultural needs and aspirations, through a jointly-owned and democratically managed company."*

The above is merely an incomplete collection of information that may have changed. Finalizing this list is a very big task; it is a movement in continuous movement and improvement.

Closing Reflections

THE BOOK POLITICAL SOLIDARITY ECONOMY CORRESPONDS TO THE EFFORT TO LEARN TO SEE REALITY AND NOT LOSE HOPE, as a type of antidote to despair.

If we take into account the long journey for communities and the broad diversity of each and every experience that exists in the world—in addition to all the energy and wisdom of humanity in the neverending search for new paths—we can understand that solidarity action is the fundamental construction to return to the sources where life is found, along with the possibility of sustaining one's self to continue walking.

Actions of solidarity also mean having the ability to give and a permanent gift that keeps on giving. In this way, what we have will become shared wealth. Therefore, our fortune is in sharing and distributing the accumulated goods. This is the true meaning of walking towards new realities, ways of living and being as a collective action.

We have to experience the impulse and shedding of our being towards this open space of beings with whom we share existence. At this moment in life the possibility of sharing appears. Through joint construction, we can grow and be free. This is the desire that guides our steps, it is the dream with which we wake up every morning, the one that makes us discover the potential of each and everyone in relation to nature to create new worlds.

Another strategic element is found in acting, i.e. seeing, feeling, thinking, and taking action. Without action, thought becomes an ideology, a sterile proposal without references. At each moment a synthesis is established of what happens anywhere in the universe and also of the peoples' collective and historical journey.

In this way, we understand the dynamics of society through our work, reflection, and action. For this reason, there is the transforming force of dialogue and thought as a product of multiple conclusions.

Thus, the reality of joining and surrendering to this ongoing movement allows us to find the paths of freedom. We are faced with the insurgency of the transforming force that comes from below, that is, from those who have been humiliated and displaced by the dominant system.

Selected Chronology

WE ARE FUELED BY THE SAME FIRE.

I believe in the importance of analyzing the facts from a chronological perspective to understand the processes, struggles, and the history of our communities and families.

When DESMI turned 30 years old (1969-1999) we produced the book *Si uno come, que coman todos: economía solidaria* (2001)[10]. At the beginning of the book, the chronology of key events in the history of DESMI is presented. As title of the book suggests, *solidarity economy*, brings together two spaces of thought that have consolidated over time.

Subsequently, we expanded the edition of the book with the history of DESMI upon completing 40 years of work (1969-2009). Chronological information was also included in the book *DESMI: memoria y esperanza* (2012)[11]. In that same period we tried to rescue the prodigious stage of Bishop Samuel Ruíz García (1960-2000).

Throughout 2013, I collaborated in the commemoration of the 40-year anniversary of the process in Chiapas for the Pastoral Congress of Mother Earth, which convened the Diocese of San Cristóbal, in reference to the First Indigenous Congress "Fray Bartolomé de Las Casas," held in San Cristóbal de Las Casas in 1974.

Likewise, I worked on a chronology together with the International Service for Peace (SIPAZ, in its Spanish acronym) in 2014 when the EZLN turned 10 years old. These processes prompted my reflections on multiple dimensions of analysis required to understand what the strategies to achieve freedom might be.

---

10   *If One Eats, May All Eat: Solidarity Economy*
11   *DESMI: Memory and Hope*

Chronology[12]

Year	Chiapas	Mexico	International
1911		November 28: Emiliano Zapata announces the Ayala Plan with the motto: Reform, Freedom, Justice and Law."	
1914			WWI begins.
1915			Genocide of more than 1 million Armenians in Turkey.
1917			The great socialist revolution begins on the night of October 24, 1917 (according to the old Russian calendar).
1934-1940		Lázaro Cárdenas' six-year presidential term.	
1943			
1944-1959	Don Lucio C. Torreblanca y Tapia, Chiapas Diocese Bishop.		The International Monetary Fund and the World Bank are established at Bretton Woods (Washington).
1945			The United Nation is established. WWII ends. On August 6th, the US drops an atomic bomb on Hiroshima (140,000 victims) On August 9th, the US drops a second atomic bomb on Nagasaki (70,000 victims)[13]
1947	Don Lucio C. Torreblanca convenes the second diocesan synod of Chiapas.		India obtains independence from the British Empire
1948			Israel is founded. May 14: UN resolution More than 800,000 Palestinians are expelled and more than 500 villages demolished. Great Britain leaves India. Decolonization process

---

12 Developed by Jorge Santiago Santiago in collaboration with Jaime Schlittler Álvarez

13 "The few survivors wandered, mutilated, sleepwalking, among the smoking ruins. They were naked and on their burns had stamped the clothes they wore when the explosion happened on their bodies. In the remains of walls, the immense fire and heat had impressed upon them the shadows of what was once before them: a woman with her arms raised, a man, a tied up horse […]" (Galeano, 2012: 252).

Year	Chiapas	Mexico	International
1951	The Tzeltal-Tzotzil Coordinating Center of the National Indigenist Institute, is created in Chiapas		
1954	Sagrado Corazón and Santa María de Guadalupe Missionaries		
1956	In 1957, the Tapachula Diocese was created. The Tuxtla Gutiérrez Diocese is created (1956), the Chiapas Diocese changes its name to the San Cristóbal de Las Casas Diocese.		
1957	The Tapachula Diocese is created.		
1959	Some religious congregations in service to the diocese configure the Chiapas Dioceses. Bachajón Jesuit Mission Franciscan Mission (Palenque and Tumbalá) Samuel Ruiz García is designated Bishop at San Cristóbal de Las Casas Bishop.		The Cuban Revolution triumphs.
1960	Colonization of the Lacandona Jungle Don Samuel's consecration as the Chiapas Bishop (1960-2000) Catechism schools begin for men (Marist brothers) and women (Sisters of the Divine Shepherd). Spring, sisters of the divine shepherd. Guadalupe mission, Marists. La Castalia Formation of pastoral teams MISED sisters[14]		
1961	Cattle law of the state of Chiapas, the creation of a federal cattle policy, the authorization for ranchers and landowners to carry arms, the declaration of ranching zones as unaffected and the suspension of land distribution in Chiapas.		Cuban people's victory at the Bay of Pigs.
1962	Catechism schools and integral formation	Rubén Jaramillo's death (Zapatista)	The Vatican Council II begins.
1963	Ocosingo Dominican Mission founded		
1964	Hydroelectric dam of Malpaso, Chipaas		The Vatican Council II ends.
1965	Presidential resolution recognizes the agrarian demands of communities in Venustiano Carranza. Father Miguel Chanteau arrives in Chenalhó. The Tuxtla Gutiérrez Diocese is created.	September 23: The Popular Guerrilla Group (GPG) assaults the Madera military, Chihuahua.	
1966	Chamula mission (Father Leopoldo Hernández)		February 15 of 1966: Camilo Torres Restrepo, a Catholic priest, pioneer of liberation theology and member of the Colombian guerrilla, is killed.

14 The diocesan secular missionaries

Year	Chiapas	Mexico	International
1967			October 9: Ché Guevara is assassinated in Bolivia. "October 8th of 1967. 1,700 soldiers ambush Ché Guevara and his few guerrilla fighters in the Yuro Ravine, Bolivia. Ché, a prisoner, was assassinated the day after" (Galeano, *2012*).
1968		Student movement protests end on October 2 with the Tlatelolco massacre. Mexican Insurgent Army forms, founded by journalist Mario Menéndez, doctor Alfredo Zárate Mota and "Justo."	Medellín Episcopal Conference
1969	The Summer Language Institute begins in multiple municipalities in Chiapas and with that the expansion of Protestantism. Father Leopoldo Hernández is expelled from Chamula. DESMI-regional Chiapas is founded.	Indigenous Encounter in Xicotepec in Juarez, Puebla. Conference between anthropologists and the National Indigenous Pastoral Center (Cenapi). On August 6 the National Liberation Forces are founded in Monterrey, Nuevo León.	July 21: astronauts walk on the moon
1970	The Velasco Suárez government begins The study of anthropology Alfonzo de Gortari Chenalhó, Mitontic Understanding of culture The experience of the pre-deacons in Ocosingo begins, after that the deaconries of the tzotzil team of the San Cristóbal de Las Casas Diocese.	The presidency of Luis Echeverría begins New phase of populist reforms	
1971	Resurgence of land invasions at Simojovel Fundación del Centro The National Indigenous Pastoral Center is founded Ach' Lecubtesel Project	Student movement repression	
1972	Creation of the Lacandona community A government decree grants 614,000 hectares of land to 66 Lacandona families, thereby displacing 2,000 Tzeltal and Ch'ol families from 26 communities, more than 71,000 people. The expulsion of Ladino people from San Andrés Larráinzar The second Tzeltal denouncement of Father Mardonio Morales E. S. J. In *Indigenous Studies*, Cenapi, vol I-III, 1971, pp.65-79, the first part is published.		Earthquake in Nicaragua

15 At 7:00 AM, Allende's last radio message: "I will not resign. I will not do it. I notify the country of the incredible attitude of soldiers that break their word and default their commitments. I make my irrevocable decision evident of continuing to defend Chile. I signal my will to resist with everything, at the expense of my life, so that the lesson is not presented in history of the remaining power of those who have force and not reason. I beseech the workers to take over their factories and to the armed forces I ask that you fulfill your constitutional duty {...}."

Year	Chiapas	Mexico	International
1973	Christians for socialism Tzeltal Denouncement by Father Mardonio Morales E.S.J. Indigenous Congress preparation Inaremac, the Mayan Region Anthropological Assessment Institute, is created		September 11: Coup d'etat in Chile deposes Salvador Allende.[15] Amílcar Cabral's assassination
1974	Indigenous congress in San Cristóbal de Las Casas: the first public manifestation of the emerging Indigenous movement On the 500th anniversary of Friar Bartolomé de Las Casas birth, more than a thousand Tzotzil, Ch'ol, Tzeltal and Tojolabal delegates gathered, and four core themes were presented: land, education, health, and commerce. "El Chilar" ranch in Ocosingo, where the guerrilla nucleus Emiliano Zapata was concentrated, is discovered; the militants that were there are assassinated and/or disappeared.	An FLN safe house is discovered in Monterrey. This information will take them to Nepantla the next day. February 14: The Armed forces attack the "Casa Grande de Nepantla," a safehouse where militants were recruited for a future expedition to the Ocosingo ranch. Six of the eight future guerilla members are assassinated: Deni Prieto Stock (María Luisa), Salvador, Manolo, Alfredo, Ricardo, Sol y Gabriel.	
1975	Municipalities in the North begin to organize and fight for land: they are shareholders of common land, petitioners, and pigeonholed "peons." Land recovery: from Villaflores to the Tzimol region, Socoltenango and Chiapa de Corzo (close to 100 farms were invaded). The San Cristóbal Diocese declares its favor towards the poor. A leftist faction of the Independent Peasant Confederation (CCI) is rebaptized as the Agrarian Workers and Peasants Independent Confederation (CIOAC). August: Bartolomé Martinez Villatoro, a Tzotzil leader, and Guadalupe Vázquez are assassinated in Venustiano Carranza. The commoners placed responsibility with ranchers Augusto Castellanos and Carmen Orantes. December 14: 60 communities, affected by the Lacandona Community Decree, create the Ejido Union Quiptic Ta Lecubtesel in the Ocosingo municipality. First Diocese Assembly. They opt in favor of the poor. In 1975, the CNC organized an Indigenous congress in Chiapas	Lucio Cabañas is assassinated.	The Vietnam revolution achieves victory. The military victory of the North united the two Vietnams (in 1973: ceasefire; in 1976: divided into two states).
1976	Army attacks the Casa del Pueblo and arrests leaders in Venustiano Carranza. Land recovery from Villa Flores to Tzimol. In Socoltenango and Chiapa de Corzo, about 100 farms are invaded (Alianza campesina, April 10).	José López Portillo presidency begins.	1976-1983: last civic-ecclesiastic-military dictatorship in Argentina. Earthquake in Guatemala.
1977	Seven policemen are killed in the common land of Providencia, in the Ocosingo municipality. The army carries out anti-guerrilla exercises in Tila. CIOAC advisors participate in the agrarian struggles in Simojovel. Federal troops are used to evict the coffee plantation land petitioners.		March 20: Father Rutilio is assassinated in El Salvador (an ally of Archbishop Romero).

Year	Chiapas	Mexico	International
1978	Guatemalan refugee migration to Chiapas begins. Imprisoned leaders are liberated in Venustiano Carranza. February: division within the Casa del Pueblo, V. Carranza. The Proletarian Line organization arrives in Chiapas		The war in Guatemala escalates. Guatemalan refugee migration begins.
1979		The National Coordinator of the Ayala Plan (CNPA) is created in Milpa Alta. The defense of land.	Sandinista triumph in Nicaragua.
1980	June: The army massacres Tzeltal people in Wololchan, Sitalá (700 families are affected). July: The Provisional Coordinator of Chiapas is created. September: The Chiapas Union of Common Land Unions and Peasant Groups in Solidarity (UU) is created. October: The "Miguel de la Cruz" Agrarian Workers Union in Simojovel is created. Between 1976 and 1980, the fight for land is direct, the evictions to dispossess farmers from their land are systematic, nevertheless, repression does not deter the strong mobilizations.		Oscar Arnulfo Romero, Archbishop of El Salvador, is assassinated (funerals on March 30). 40 Mayan Quiché people are assassinated at the Spanish Embassy in Guatemala. Beginning of the war in El Salvador.
1980	The state government is forced to buy and distribute various occupied properties. In the 1980s, more than 80,000 hectares are distributed among roughly a thousand peasants that in turn found ejidos.		
1981	April: arrest and imprisonment of Arturo Albores Velasco and Victórico Martínez-Hernández in Venustiano Carranza. CIOAC organizes strikes at the coffee plantations of Simojovel to demand that it be recognized as a local union. October: a massive UU demonstration in Tuxtla Gutiérrez (the Union of Unions). 45,000 soldiers carry out anti-guerrilla maneuvers and simulations in the Ch'ol region (Tila and Sabanilla) in the Jungle border. Military observers from Guatemala participate.	May: Massive manifestation by the CNPA and teachers' democratic movement in Mexico City. August: hunger strike organized by the CNPA for the liberation of peasants imprisoned due to agrarian struggles.	
1982	"Interinstitutional Plan for Economic Development" and the "Industrial Stimulation Plan" for Chiapas. The PRI chooses a military official as governor of Chiapas: General Absalón Castellanos Dominguez, one of the most powerful ranchers of the region, his governance was one of history's most difficult and tragic. New peasant organizations emerge, that represented a deep and widespread discontent, such as the total lack of trust in official organizations. The sit-ins, land invasions, manifestations, denouncements in forums and encounters were permanent throughout these years until 1985.	Mexican economic crisis Miguel de la Madrid presidency Since 1982, neoliberalism's implementation	Malvinas War[16]

Year	Chiapas	Mexico	International
1982	Repression was systemic. During Absalón Castellanos' governance, 153 assassinations were carried out in Chiapas, 692 imprisonments, 327 disappeared peasants, 407 families expelled from their communities, and 54 displacements of entire populations. Hundreds of Zoque Indigenous peoples were killed by the Chichonal Volcano eruption. Division between the principal factions in the Union of Unions July: the Chiapas Provisional Coordinator was rebaptized as the Emiliano Zapata Peasant Organization (OCEZ). Guatemalan refugees The formation of organizations Harvey Carmen Legorreta's book Cristina Renard's book on the Venustiano Carranza Casa del Pueblo Juan Gonzalez Esponda's book: *The Chiapas Zapatistas*. Furthermore, his thesis "The peasant movement in the September 28 organization" The book about Arturo Albores Velasco, assassinated in Chiapas on March 6, 1989: *To the Other World* by Maricela González Jurado. Assembly meeting of the Union of Unions in San Miguel, Ocosingo		
1983	May: The Chiapas Plan is announced. Marie Odile Marion Singer's *The 1983 Chiapas Peasant Movement* October: CIOAC march from Chiapas to Mexico City Members of the National Liberation Forces (FLN) arrive in the Lacandona Jungle November 17: a group made up of six people– the first six insurgents, 5 men and 1 woman, of which 3 were mestizos and 3 Indigenous– form, somewhere in the jungle, the second guerrilla concentration Emiliano Zapata, father-mother of the Zapatista Army for National Liberation (EZLN). A key year in relation to the founding of a coalition: OCEZ, CIOAC, Union of Unions, the beginning of the EZLN, etc.		
1984	The Chiapas Highlands Indigenous Representatives Council (CRIACH) is formed, along with representatives of the settlements and colonies of displaced people living in San Cristóbal and Teopisca. The state government announces the Agrarian Rehabilitation Program (PRA). Divisions within the OCEZ due to leadership and alliances. Nine members of the Casa del Pueblo are ambushed and killed in Venustiano Carranza. In the 80s, at the San Cristóbal de Las Casas Diocese, the women's pastoral looked to promote peasant women in their families, communities and organizations from a committed religiosity.		More than 37,000 people are estimated to have died since 1984, when the armed group led by Abdullah Öcalan, known as "Apo" by his followers, began a bloody campaign in Turkey for the recognition of rights for oppressed Kurdish people.

Year	Chiapas	Mexico	International
1984	Read God's word from the position of women. In 1984, in the Chiapas Autonomous University's Social Science School, the research workshop about the Anzetik woman[17] was created.		
1985		Mexico City earthquake and social mobilization. The National Union of Autonomous Regional Peasant Organizations (UNORCA) is formed. Division in the CNPA over the role of political parties in the peasant movement.	
1986	Judicial police and chiefs in the service of Enrique Zardaín and Astrid Astudillo burn and raze to the ground 50 houses in Muc'ulum, Bachajón, Chilón municipality for the second time. Peasant women from the south conferences.	Corn producers protest, in alliance with the teachers' democratic movement.	
1987	The Mexican Unified Socialist Party (PSUM) reported that between 1974 and 1987, in 11 municipality's in the north of the state, there were 27 displacements, 19 attempted displacements, 47 peasants assassinated, 160 wounded, 205 imprisoned, 92 kidnapped and tortured, and 8 women raped. March: agreement to create the Coordinating Committee for the Preservation of the Lacandona Jungle.		
1988	Creation of the EZLN's CCRI. Representatives from the 7 ethnicities that make up the EZLN, Tzotzil, Tzeltal, Tojolabal, Ch'ol, Mame, Zoque and mestiza, will create an ample structure through which they will provide political direction for the rebel army.	Electoral fraud against Cuauhtémoc Cardenas. Carlos Salinas de Gortari takes the presidency of the Republic (1988-1994)	
1989	Creation of the "Friar Bartolomé de Las Casas" Center for Human Rights of CIAM, CIDECI, and Chiltak. The formation of organizations in Chiapas John Womack	Restructuration of the Mexican Coffee Institute (Inmecafé) November: the Salinas government announces reforms to Article 27 of the federal constitution. The Agrarian Development Law is promoted with the attempt to put an end to land distribution.	The Berlin Wall falls. World coffee prices fall.
1990	Patrocinio González Garrido is governor of Chiapas	Carlos Salinas de Gortari delivered the definitive plan to the indigenous community Venustiano Carranza, which protects more than 50,000 hectares according to the 1965 presidential decree.	

17 Tzeltal woman.

Year	Chiapas	Mexico	International
1991	February 25: relevant to agrarian concerns, the Río Florido ejido in the Ocosingo municipality (now OCEZ-FSLN) is founded. March 31: pastoral document about abortion from Bishop Samuel Ruíz García. September18: Father Joel's imprisonment. Emergence of faithful people. Pilgrimage to demand the release of Father Joel. July: The Emiliano Zapata National Alliance of Independent Peasants (ANCIEZ) is created. The process of analysis of reality An understanding of reality that emerges from the confrontation of interests.		"On Christmas eve of 1991, the Soviet Union died and in the process Russian capitalism was born" (Galeano 2012: 402)
1992	Xi Nich March from Palenque to the capital. October 12: March for Indigenous Dignity due to 500 years of exploitation. After various municipal mobilizations, 25 organizations, grouped through the Chiapas Social Organizations Front organized a large march in San Cristóbal de Las Casas. Their demands were: "no to the TLC," "no to article 27 reforms," "enough of 500 years." More than 10,000 Indigenous people participated. Large confrontation between the church and state in Chiapas. December: Creation of the social organization, the Bees for the liberation of the 5 imprisoned of Tzajach'en. Confirmation of a specific pastoral labor with women from the word of God, with a diocesan coordinator: Women Diocesan Coordinator (Codimuj).	February: the Mexican congress implements the new Agrarian Law. Article 27 constitutional reforms, referencing agrarian reform. Reform resulted in the debilitation of the ejido and communal land system. Manifestations against the 5th Centennial of the "discovery" of America. Diplomatic relationships between the Holy Headquarters and the Mexican government are established.	Signing of the Peace Agreements in El Salvador.
1993	In March, the 31st military zone command reported that a Mexican Air Force captain and an army sergeant were assassinated and later burned on land belonging to the community of San Isidro El Ocotal, San Cristóbal de Las Casas municipality. They imprisoned 13 suspects from the community. In May, the federal army finds an insurgent training camp close to La Garrucha (Las calabazas), and various military officers die there, but these events are practically silenced in the shadow of the imminent signing of the Free Trade Agreement between the United States and Canada, underestimating the rebel army. Secretary of State: Patrocinio González Garrido Women's Revolutionary Law (EZLN) El Prado (Accord) Don Samuel presents his pastoral letter "In This Hour of Grace" to the Pope. A survey of Zapatista communities is carried out concerning the decision to go or not go to war against the government and the army.	Intense federal and state campaign to advance and concretize the "certification of parcel rights" (privatization of ejido parcels) based on the article 27 constitutional reform. Intense federal and state campaign to advance and specify the "Certification of Parcelary Rights" (privatization of ejidal plots) based on the reform of the constitutional Article 27.	Peace accords are signed in El Salvador

Year	Chiapas	Mexico	International
1994	Armed EZLN uprising. Seven municipal seats are taken, confrontations with the army and police in different areas. Dialogue between the EZLN and the federal government at the San Cristóbal cathedral. On January 1, the EZLN declares war against the federal government and its army and begins to occupy several municipalities. From the first days of initiating the conflict, national and international civil society backs a political and peaceful solution. By July, organized Indigenous women in artisanal and productive cooperatives (such as J'pas Joloviletick, OIMI, J'pas Lumetic, Nan Choch and Isman), belonging to Indigenous and peasant organizations (such as CIOAC, Anipa and Oriach) and connected to health projects (CSESC and OMIECH), along with mestiza consultants from feminist non-governmental organizations (such as COLEM, CIAM, and K'inal Antzetik), had begun to create an expansive women's front, and their first mobilization was the State Convention of Chiapan Women. On January 12, multiple manifestations for peace across the whole country were held. On this day, the EZLN and the federal government enter into a unilateral ceasefire due to pressure from national and international civil society. Emergence of CONAI. From October 13, 1994 to June 7, 1998. Don Samuel's mediation. Peace with justice and dignity. Don Samuel, as mediator, begins fasting for peace. January: The State Council of Indigenous and Peasant Organizations (CEOIC) is formed with 280 social and economic organizations. February-March: Dialogue between the EZLN and government representatives in the San Cristóbal de Las Casas cathedral, mediated by Don Samuel Ruíz García.	The Free Trade Agreement between the United States, Canada and Mexico is vigorously implemented. Thousands of people from national and international civil society mobilize to evade war. March 23: Colosio, PRI presidential candidate is assassinated: Ernesto Zedillo will take over that role and will win the presidential elections. At the end of the year, in midst of rumors and fears, one of the largest financial crises in the history of the country occurs.	

Year	Chiapas	Mexico	International
1994	Civil society actively participates in The Peace Ribbon Campaign.		
	The cathedral dialogues end with various government proposals.		
	The EZLN, on the other hand, announces that they will consult with the Zapatista bases about them.		
	June: the EZLN base rejects the government proposals to carry out reforms in Chiapas, given that 98% of the base considered that these proposals do not address the original causes of the conflict.		
	June 10: Second Lacandona Jungle declaration.		
	August 8: The Democratic National Convention is held in Aguascalientes de Guadalupe Tepeyac.		
	The EZLN decides to maintain the ceasefire and continue dialogues with civil society. It convenes the National Democratic Convention.		
	August 6 to 9: The National Democratic Convention is held with the participation of six thousand representatives from social and civil organizations from throughout Mexico.		
	August 21: Fraudulent elections in Chiapas hand over a victory to PRI candidate, Eduardo Robledo.		
	The State Assembly of the Chiapan People, the Chiapan People Electoral Attorney General, the Chiapan People Electoral Tribunal and the Popular Jury come together.		
	In October, Don Samuel launches an initiative for a new dialogue, which includes an expansion of the mediation with members from civil society.		
	Autonomous municipalities.		
	On December 19, Operation peace with justice and dignity for indigenous peoples.		
	The EZLN breaks through the military perimeter imposed by the Mexican army and takes over 38 municipal seats without using violence, declaring all them autonomous rebel municipalities.		
	Amado Avendaño assumes his role as "governor in rebellion."		

Year	Chiapas	Mexico	International
1995	January 1: Third declaration of the Lancadona Jungle. The Mexican government takes over the Guadalupe Tepeyac community. The intense state militarization process begins. In April, EZLN delegates, the federal government, and CONAI come together at the San Miguel ejido, Ocosingo municipality, to talk and agree on the dialogue process. August: the EZLN launches a national and international consultation to define the future of their struggle. More than a million people responded. Most supported the transformation of the EZLN into a political force in a new way. October: the San Andrés Larráinzar talks begin again, supported by Bishop Raúl Vera. While the San Andrés talks are happening, the federal government begins to develop and apply its counterinsurgency strategy in the northern jungle zone (Tumbalá, Sabanilla, Tila, Salto de Agua). First conference on the future and the solidarity economy.	February 9: the federal government changes strategy, President Zedillo orders a new military offensive against the EZLN and new orders are issued for the arrest of those believed to belong to the Zapatista leadership. On March 11, the Union's Congress approves the Dialogue, Conciliation and Dignified Peace in Chiapas Law. The Harmony and Pacification Commission (Cocopa) is formed to help in the negotiations, legislators from all political parties represented in Congress are part of it.	
1996	On January 1, 1996 the Zapatista Front for National Liberation (FZLN) was born. Fourth Lacandona Jungle declaration. In January, 300 Indigenous representatives, from at least 35 communities across the country, come together at the National Indigenous Forum. The participants agree to create the Indigenous National Congress (CNI). On February 16, after five months of negotiations, the government and the EZLN sign the first accords over Indigenous rights and culture in San Andrés, known as the "San Andrés accords". From July 27 to August 3, the EZLN celebrates the Intercontinental Reunion for Humanity and Against Neoliberalism in the Zapatista Aguascalientes. September: the EZLN suspends its participation in the peace talks, until the San Andrés accords were implemented along with other demands. There are organized paramilitary groups supported by the PRI in the north and the center of Chiapas. Low intensity warfare grows in Chiapas. Creation of the Commission to Support Unity and Community Reconciliation (Coreco). Due to governmental lack of follow through, the dialogue and negotiation enter in a new and prolonged crisis. Many organizations in Chiapas resume their trajectories once more. October 12: Creation of the Indigenous National Congress under the motto "never again a Mexico without us."		Guatemalan peace accords

Year	Chiapas	Mexico	International
1997	In January, the EZLN accuses the government of not respecting the agreements, as they presented a different proposal to the Cocopa Law. Throughout the entire year, the EZLN and other organizations carry out protests to achieve the implementation of the San Andrés accords. Innumerable practices of autonomy begin in Zapatista zones. In Chiapas, the counterinsurgency strategy grows and gravely imposes violence in the life of communities. December 22: Paramilitaries assassinate 45 Zapatista sympathizers, members of the Bees in Acteal, Chenalhó. The resistance The autonomous municipalities The pluriethnic autonomous regions OCEZ The EPR Political parties The magisterial movement The peasant movement Yachil Antzetic Serapaz INESIN		*The Black Radical Congress* Campaign for the liberation of Mumia Abu-Jamal
1998	A new phase of the counterinsurgency strategy is launched through political and military vehicles in the media, and through attacks and expulsions of solidarity groups. June 7: Bishop Samuel Ruiz announces the CONAI's dissolution as a denouncement of the situation, more than a resignation. Mediation for peace with justice and dignity began in 1994 with Don Samuel's first intervention with the Cathedral dialogues. Meanwhile, militarization continues to run high. Police-military operatives multiply in great numbers against the Zapatista autonomous municipalities: Flores Magón in April, Tierra y Libertad in May, San Juan de la Libertad in June. In Chiapas, the new governor Roberto Albores Guillén launches a great offensive to re-establish what he considers the State's rights. Diocesan synod Deaconed directory July 17: Fifth Lacandona Jungle declaration	Indigenous law initiatives multiply, one from the PRI supports President Zedillo, another from the PAN, among others. This diminishes the possibilities that the Cocopa text, accepted by the EZLN, be considered by the Union Congress. Crisis in the state party October 22 to November 5: Hurricane Mitch[18]	Archbishop Gerardi is assassinated in Guatemala.

18   Hurricane Mitch was one of the most powerful and deadly cyclones that have been seen in the modern era, with a maximum velocity of 290km/hr. The affected areas were Nicaragua, Honduras, Yucatan Peninsula, Florida and Central America.

Year	Chiapas	Mexico	International
1999	Federal army invasion of the Amador Hernández, Chiapas ejido. The government says that the conflict is only happening in Chiapas and in four municipalities of the state. This statement seeks to ease issues with development programs and makes it so they do not have to consult or dialogue with the Zapatistas. March 21: Five thousand delegates leave Aguascalientes and head to 32 states around the country to convene the national consultation for the recognition of Indigenous peoples rights and for the end of the war of extermination. October 14: JCanan Lum, a name given to Don Samuel by Indigenous communities in Amatenango del Valle, Chiapas.[19] The end of the third synod. Deacon ordinations in Huixtán.		Antiglobalization protests in Seattle, Washington, United States.
2000	Don Samuel Ruíz García reaches 40 years of service as Bishop and becomes Bishop Emeritus. June 12: Seven uniformed people were ambushed and assassinated in El Bosque. The EPR was accused, paramilitaries and Zapatistas. The PGJE also blamed Salvador López. A week later, professor Alberto Patishtán Gómez was detained (June 19). Pablo Salazar Mendiguchía, with the support and the hope of a large number of organizations and communities in Chiapas, assumes the role of the state government as part of the PRD. Strengthening of the evangelical movements to reach God's army. In December, after months of silence and without having participated in the elections, the Zapatistas hold a press conference recognizing that the new governments could be a new opportunity for peace. They ask for three signs to reconvene dialogue: the implementation of the San Andrés accords, the liberation of Zapatista prisoners, and the closing down of seven military bases located in the area of maximum Zapatista influence (of the existing 289). They announce a march to Mexico D.F. to defend the proposal for constitution reform redacted by the Cocopa, based on the San Andrés accords.	Federal elections of July 2 mark a historical change in Mexico. After 71 years, the PRI loses the presidency and Vicente Fox of the PAN wins (2000-2006).	
2001	March-April: Zapatistas carry out the March for the Color of the Earth to the D.F. to defend the legal initiative for Indigenous rights developed by COCOPA in 1996. The EZLN returns to resistance and silence. They put into practice autonomy through action and they reject state and federal government programs. They reinforce military and vigilante forces in Chiapas, especially on the Guatemalan border, the northern zone and other strategic places.	In April, the Union Congress approves a different Indigenous law, not the one developed by COCOPA. The government says that there is peace and tranquility in Chiapas and with the Zapatistas, and that the Indigenous law that has been approved is one of the best in Latin America. Furthermore, it begins to promote development through plans such as the Puebla Panama Plan (PPP).	September 11: Attack on the Twin Towers in New York and the Pentagon in Washington, D.C.

19   Juan Manuel Hurtado calls for a ritual of consecration of Jtatic Samuel as JCanan Lum. "From now on, you are now ready, you have power before all enemies, no matter how large they are, to defend your people; you have wisdom, you come from God, in you lives a great nagual to serve your people; with forty years of service for your people you already demonstrated your strength, your wisdom. This is why we name you and consecrate you as JCanan Lum, "the caretaker of your people," "he who loves and defends it," you have the power to do that, you are in the prime of life." This is how the principal, the elder, the community wise man talked to Don Samuel in the name of the Tzeltal people and of all the peoples represented.

Year	Chiapas	Mexico	International
2002	From April to December, the EZLN is silent.		
2003	January 1, the EZLN breaks its silence. More than 20 thousand Indigenous people take over the city of San Cristóbal, the largest concentrated support for the EZLN to date.	In July, elections for federal representatives are held. The largest abstentionism percentage (60%) in the history of the country is recorded.	
	In Chiapas, electoral abstention is the highest in all of Mexico.		
	Simultaneously, the EZLN announces a series of changes that refers to its internal functioning and its relationship with national and international civil society (seven documents that make up the 13th Stellae).		
	In an action celebrated in Oventik from August 8 to 10, the EZLN command announces the disappearance of Aguascalientes, the creation of the Caracoles and the Good Government Juntas (JBG) to install their autonomy established in the San Andrés accords.		
	The EZLN announces the withdrawal of checkpoints and tolls along highways and road tolls throughout the territories under its control, as a gesture of good will toward communities that are not Zapatistas. Nevertheless, the EZLN will continue to work for the defense of the autonomous municipalities.		
	The creation of the JBG implies that relationships will change, both inside and outside of the Zapatista territories.		
2004	January 25: Don Samuel presented his pastoral letter "a new hour of grace."		
2005	May: The sixth Lacandona Jungle declaration is launched.	April 7: More than 330,000 people protest against the disqualification of Andrés Manuel López Obrador.	April 2: John Paul II, the leader of more than a billion Catholics throughout the world dies at 84.
	The EZLN launches The Other Campaign.	April 24: The silent march with more than a million people.	April 19: New pope, Joseph Ratzinger (78 years old), Benedict XVI.
2006	January 1: The first phase of The Other Campaign begins.	May 4: State and federal forces forcefully repress San Salvador Atenco.	United Nations Declaration on the Rights of Indigenous Peoples. In June 2006, it was approved by the Commission on Human Rights and in September 2007, by the General Assembly.
	Juan Sabines Gutiérrez, governor of the State of Chiapas	In June, APPO is created in Oaxaca.	
	Emergence of organizational processes to negotiate with the government, a vast number of projects. Resistance to PROCEDE. Resistance to electricity payments. Organizations that maintain a pact with the government. Processes in defense of territory. FNLS is founded. The Other Campaign Autonomous municipalities Attack groups Paramilitaries Religious organizations	Electoral fraud against Andrés Mauel López Obrador. Felipe Calderón Hinojosa, president of Mexico	

Year	Chiapas	Mexico	International
2007	March 25: The second phase of The Other Campaign is launched. September 20: Andrés Aubry dies. December 2007-January 2008: "The First International Colloquium *In remembrance of Andrés Aubry.*" " […] Planet earth: Anti-system movements […]"	Between July 5 and 10: Eight explosives were detonated in the oil ducts located in Guanajuato and Querétaro. The Popular Revolutionary Army (EPR) claimed responsibility for these actions, affirming that they are part of a campaign against the government of Felipe Calderón to demand the return of two of four of its disappeared politicians in Oaxaca on May 25, Gabriel Alberto Cruz Sánchez and Edmundo Ramírez Amaya.	
2008	Between February and April, a historic protest of hunger strikes by detainees who declared themselves to be political prisoners and asked for their immediate liberation, occurred in different jails in Chiapas and one in Tabasco. This process allowed the release of more than 100 people from different detention centers in Chiapas. December 2008-January 2009: the EZLN holds the World Festival of Righteous Rage in D.F. And Chiapas.		
2009	On August 12: the National Supreme Court (SCJN) issued a vote in favor of pardoning and freeing 20 of the paramilitaries that perpetrated the Acteal massacre.		
2010	The InterAmerican Commission for Human Rights accepted the Acteal case. Six years after the Acteal case presentation, the CIDH responds to the historical debt of justice. JCanan Lum Don Samuel agreed with establishing this recognition, taking into account the responsibility that the Indigenous communities gave him as the "caretaker of the people". Pastoral theological congress Jtatic Samuel Museum proposal. The Faithful People Pilgrimage of November 19. December 2010-January 2011: First Planet Earth Reflection and Analysis Seminar, anti-system movements, CIDECI-Unitierra	Mechanisms of control by the government The counterinsurgency The Calderón War Land conflicts	

Year	Chiapas	Mexico	International
	May 7: Zapatista march in support related to the Movement for peace with justice and dignity (EZLN communiqué).		
	Correspondence between Subcommander Marcos and Don Luis Villoro		
	Felipe Toussaint dies.		
	Javier Sicilia movement due to the assassination of his son in April (Javier Sicilia communiqué)		
	Javier Sicilia convocation		
	November 26: Pilgrimage of faithful people and ecclesiastical base communities.		
	EZLN communiqué announcement		
	Organized civil society		
	December 2011-January 2012: Second Planet Earth Reflection and Analysis Seminar, anti-system movements, CIDECI-Unitierra		
2012	The silent EZLN march	Enrique Peña Nieto, President	
	December 21: 17 years after the failure to fulfill the San Andrés accords.		
	Manuel Velasco Coello, governor of the State of Chiapas		
	December 2012-January 2013: Third Planet Earth Reflection and Analysis Seminar, anti-system movements, CIDECI-Unitierra.		
	February 20: Victoria Espejo Villalobos dies, *compañera*, friend, sibling, and sister of the congregation of San José de Lyon.		
2013	January 25: Pilgrimage of the faithful	A political pact by the parties and the reforms driven by the Enrique Peña Nieto government.	Benedict XVI resigns; Pope Francisco is elected.
	Pastoral pre-congresses for the earth, convened and organized by the San Cristóbal Diocese.	The National Crusade Against Hunger	
	EZLN communiqué announcements.		
	Grouping of communiqués published by Beatriz Aurora.		
	"La Escuelita" convening		
	"The forces of silence 12-21-12"		
	The EZLN announces its next steps.		
	Eón Editions		
	August: First round of the little Zapatista school		
	10th anniversary of the Caracoles and the JBG		
	The Tata Chávez Alonso Chair for the refounding of the CNI		
	October 31: Alberto Patishtán liberation		

Year	Chiapas	Mexico	International
2014	The pastoral congress for the earth. May: Subcommander Marcos' death. August 2014: Second declaration of CNI-EZLN about our peoples' dispossession. December 2013-January 2014: Second and third round of the little Zapatista school	September 26: Ayotzinapa, Guerrero State, disappearance of 43 students, 6 people executed extrajudicially, and 25 wounded. Actions perpetrated by the Iguala municipal police, under the orders of the municipal president in alliance with organized crime. From November 11 to 13: Mexico, D.F., final hearing of the TPP.	
2015	May: "The Crack in the Wall," first notebook about the Zapatista method. Report from the Center for Human Rights, Fray Bartolomé de Las Casas, A.C. "The Reality, A Context of War." "Critical thought against the Capitalist Hydra" seminar to be celebrated from May 3-9 of 2015, begins at the Oventik Caracol and continues at CIDECI in San Cristóbal de Las Casas, Chiapas.	From December 21, 2014 to January 2, 2015: The first global festival for resistance and rebellion against capitalism. Event convened by the CNI and the EZLN.	March 25: Creation of the *Global University for Sustainability* (GUS) in Tunisia during the World Social Forum.[8]

References

◇◇

THERE ARE MANY RESOURCES AND WRITINGS ABOUT THE SOLIDARITY ECONOMY. Thus, I consider the Intercontinental Network of Social Solidarity Economy (RIPESS, in its Spanish acronym), of greater relevance given its significance in Canada and Latin America for its role in building this information network and promoting social and solidarity economy. Likewise, there are various sources of information in which different research and analytical works have been published, meaning that each region of the world has a history in the construction process. In Chiapas, for example, we learned to build with the autonomy and resistance of indigenous communities, hence, it is important to understand solidarity economy within the context of land defense, strategic resources and the rights of indigenous communities; in reference to the San Andrés Accords concerning indigenous rights and culture (1996).

From 2001 to 2008, the institution for the Social Economic Development of Indigenous Mexicans (DESMI, in its Spanish acronym) held eight annual solidarity economy meetings in San Cristóbal de las Casas, Chiapas, with the participation of representatives from different autonomous communities in Chiapas and from Mexico in general, along with communities from Guatemala, El Salvador, Nicaragua, Haiti, Italy, France, Spain, the United States, Canada, the UK, Belgium, Holland, Switzerland, Norway and Japan. It was a sampling of what was taking place in the world.

DESMI has been in Chiapas since 1969, taking its first steps alongside Indigenous and farming communities. Its lines of work are economic action, supporting the initiatives of the communities with administrative advice, programming, analysis, and agroecological technologies. In collaboration with communities, DESMI has been discovering the strategic objectives for which it is necessary to organize and work, such as the construction of a solidarity economy. To fulfill its mission, DESMI has been supported by international development cooperation agencies for 30 years.

With regard to the experience of Zapatista communities, there are also various studies, information and reflection on the construction of alternatives with one's own effort in a context of counterinsurgency and war, and on how the practice of alternatives becomes the building of Indigenous people's autonomy. (see Cristina Híjar González and Juan E. García, *Zapatista Autonomy, Another World is Possible*).

Bibliography

Attali, Jacques (2010), "Presentación." *El hombre nómada*, Bogotá, Colombia: Luna Libros.

Baronnet, Bruno, Mora Bayo, Mariana y Stahler-Sholk, Richard (editors) (2011). *Luchas, "muy otras". Zapatismo y autonomía en las comunidades indígenas de Chiapas.* México: CIESAS/UAm-Xochimilco/Uach.

Baschet, Jérome (2013). *Haciendo otros mundos. Autogobierno, sociedad del buen vivir, multiplicidad de los mundos.* San Cristóbal de Las Casas, Chiapas. México: Ediciones Cideci-Unitierra.

Bedoya, Carolina y Clayton Conn (2014). *En la celebración del 25 aniversario del Centro de Derechos Humanos "Fray Bartolomé de Las Casas."* March 17-19, 2014.

Boff, Leonardo (1966). *Grito de la tierra, grito de los pobres. Hacia una ecología planetaria.* México, D. F.: Ediciones Dabar.

Cedillo, Adela (2008). *El fuego y el silencio, historia de las FPL (Fuerzas patrióticas de Liberación).* México: Comité 68 pro Libertades Democráticas, A. C.

Cerda García, Alejandro (2011). "Entrevista a José Luis, Consejo autónomo, 3 de agosto de 2003." En la tesis *Imaginando zapatismo: Multiculturalidad y autonomía indígena en Chiapas desde un municipio autónomo.*

Coraggio, José Luis (1992). "Del sector informal a la economía popular: un paso estratégico para el planteamiento de alternativas populares de desarrollo social." ponencia presentada en el seminario-taller *Integración y desarrollo alternativo en América Latina*, organizado por el Encuentro de partidos y movimientos políticos del Foro de Sao Paulo, Lima, Perú.

Coraggio, José Luis (1999). "¿Competir por el capital o competir por la gente?" Ponencia en el seminario *Internacional Grandes metrópolis del mercosur: problemas y desafíos*, organizado por el Instituto de Estudios Urbanos de la Pontificia Universidad Católica de Chile, Santiago de Chile.

Coraggio, José Luis (2002). "La economía social como vía para otro desarrollo social." Documento de lanzamiento del debate sobre Distintas propuestas de economía social en urbared. Red de políticas Sociales. Accessed via <www.urbared.ungs.educar>.

Coraggio, José Luis (2003). "Alternativas en la lucha contra la pobreza y la exclusión." Exposición invitada como experto internacional en la sesión plenaria del eje 3 Lucha contra la pobreza y la exclusión del Diálogo Nacional. Quito, Ecuador.

Coraggio, José Luis (2008). "La economía social y solidaria como estrategia de desarrollo en el contexto de la integración regional latinoamericana." Ponencia presentada en el Tercer Encuentro Latinoamericano de Economía Solidaria y Comercio Justo organizado por RIPESS en Montevideo October 22-24, 2008.

DESMI, A. C. (2001). *Si uno come que coman todos. Economía solidaria*. México.

DESMI, A. C. (2001-2008). *8 encuentros de economía solidaria.*

DESMI, A. C. (2001-2008). *Encuentros de mujeres.*

DESMI, A. C. (2012). *DESMI: memoria y esperanza. 40 años de experiencias de acompañamiento en la construcción de autonomía con las comunidades indígenas y campesinas de Chiapas. 1969-2009.* México: DESMI, A. C.

DESMI, A. C. (2012). *Encuentro de intercambio de experiencias sobre agricultura sostenible y soberanía alimentaria*. San Cristóbal de las Casas, Chiapas, México.

DESMI, A.C. (2013). *Segundo Encuentro Internacional de agricultura sostenible, soberanía alimentaria y economía solidaria*. San Cristóbal de Las Casas, Chiapas, México.

Dierckxsens, Wim (1998). "Por un paradigma alternativo ante un neoliberalismo sin perspectiva." *Pasos*, No. 76, March-April. San José, Costa Rica: Departamento Ecuménico de Investigaciones.

Enlace, Comunicación y Capacitación, A. C. (2006). *Una aproximación a la Economía Solidaria: aportes desde experiencias de construcción local en las Cañadas de la Selva Lacandona, Chiapas*. México: Enlace, Comunicación y Capacitación, A. C.

EZLN (2013). *La fuerza del silencio 21-12-12*. México: Eón

EZLN (2014). *Cuadernos de texto de primer grado del curso de La libertad según los (las) zapatistas: Gobierno autónomo I, Gobierno autónomo II, Resistencia autónoma, participación de las mujeres en el gobierno autónomo.*

Galeano, Eduardo (2012). *Los hijos de los días*. México: Siglo XXI. García de León, Antonio (2002). *Fronteras interiores. Chiapas: una modernidad particular*. México: Océano.

Gasparello, Giovanna y Quintana Guerrero, Jaime (editors) (2009). *Otras geografías. Experiencias de autonomías indígenas en México."* México: UAm.

González Marín, Adelina (2013). "DESMI: una construcción del otro desarrollo en Chiapas." Tesis, México.

González-Ponciano, Jorge Ramón (1998). *Esas sangres no están limpias: el racismo, el Estado y la nación en Guatemala (1944-1997)*. Separata del anuario 1997. México: Centro de Estudios Superiores de México y Centroamérica/Gobierno del Estado de Chiapas/Universidad de Ciencias y Artes de Chiapas.

Grupo Red de Economía Solidaria del Perú (GRESP). *Otra economía acontece en Latinoamérica y Caribe*, Lima, Perú.

Guimont Marceau, Stéphane (2006). *Memoire: Autonomie et Développement territorial au Mexique zapatiste: La part des organisations sociales*. Montréal, Canada: Universidad de Quebec.

Harvey, Neil (2001). *La rebelión de Chiapas, la lucha por la tierra y la democracia*. México: Era.

Hernández Navarro, Luis (2002). "La paz lejana", *La Jornada*. p. 21, April 30. Chiapas.

Hernández Navarro, Luis (2013). *Siembra de concreto, cosecha de ira*. México: Centro de estudios para el cambio en el campo mexicano y para leer en libertad, A. C.

Híjar González, Cristina y Juan E. García (2008). *Autonomía zapatista, otro mundo es posible*. Accessed via <www.autonomiazapatista.com>.

Le Bot, Yvon (2013). *La gran revuelta indígena*, México: Editorial Océano.

Mance, Euclides André (2006). *Redes de colaboración solidaria—aspectos económico-filosóficos: complejidad y liberación*, México D. F.: UACm.

Marañón Pimentel, Boris (editor) (2013). *La economía solidaria en México*, México: Universidad Nacional Autónoma de México/Instituto de Investigaciones Económicas.

Martínez Rodríguez, Jorge (2013). *Otro mundo es posible y necesario, ¿cómo lograrlo?* Guadalajara, Jalisco, México.

Mendoza Hernández, Antonio (2013). "Del desarrollo alternativo a alternativas al desarrollo. Un horizonte en el buen vivir." Ponencias del Congreso Internacional Economía, Crecimiento y Desarrollo, Facultad de Ciencias Sociales, San Cristóbal de Las Casas, Chiapas, México.

Meyer, Jean (2000). *Samuel Ruiz en San Cristóbal 1960-2000*. México: Tusquets editores.

Minerva, Francesca (2008). *Camminare domandando. Il movimento zapatista e il progetto Tatawelo*. Italia: Libero mondo et Associazione Tatawelo.

Montemayor, Carlos (2002). "Más allá de los vasallos." *Proceso*, No. 1330, pp. 22-23, April 28.

Mora Bayo, Mariana (2008). "Decolonizing Politics: Zapatista Indigenous Autonomy in an Era of Neoliberal Governance and Low Intensity Warfare." Doctoral Thesis in Philosophy, University of Austin, Texas.

Plataforma de Agricultura Sostenible (2007). *La verdadera economía: la economía solidaria*. El Salvador.

Polito, Elizabeth y Juan González Esponda (1996). "Cronología. Veinte años de conflictos en el campo: 1974-1993." *Revista Chiapas*, No. 2, pp. 197-220, México: Era.

Razeto M., Luis (1993). *De la economía popular a la economía de solidaridad en un proyecto de desarrollo alternativo*. México: Imdosoc.

Razeto, Luis (1993). "De la economía popular a la economía de solidaridad, en un proyecto de desarrollo alternativo." México: Instituto Mexicano de Doctrina Social Cristiana.

Razeto, Luis (2001). "La economía comprensiva. Un proceso de desarrollo completamente diferente. El problema de la limitación de los recursos en el mundo." Accessed via <www.Luis Razeto.net>.

Ruíz García, Samuel (1993). "En esta hora de gracia" (carta pastoral).

Rus, Jean (2009), "La lucha contra los caciques indígenas en los Altos de Chiapas. Disidencia, Religión y Exilio en Chamula. 1969-1977." *Anuario de Estudios Indígenas XIII*, pp. 181-230.

Salgado, Juan (1997). *DESMI: trazando el camino hacia la economía solidaria*. México: Academia mexicana de Derechos Humanos.

Santiago Santiago, Jorge (2001). "Chiapas 2001", *Revista Subjetividad y Cultura*. No. 16, April, México.

Santiago Santiago, Jorge (2004). "Sujet et développement local au Chiapas: témoignages et réflexions", *Hégoa, Développement local et sujet géographique*, No. 25, France.

Santiago Santiago, Jorge (2009). "Construcción de alternativas en las prácticas pequeñas: Economía solidaria." *Otras Geografías. Experiencias de autonomías indígenas en México*, Giovanna Gasparello y Jaime Quintana Guerrero (editors), UAm-Iztapalapa.

Santiago Santiago, Jorge (2010). "Les pratiques de l'économie solidaire dans les communautés autonomes du Chiapas au Mexique." *Vie Economique*, Vol.1, No. 3, Canadá.

Schlittler Álvarez, Jaime (2012). ¿LekilKuxlejal como horizonte de lucha? Una reflexión colectiva sobre la autonomía en Chiapas. San Cristóbal de Las Casas, Chiapas, México: Centro de Investigaciones y Estudios Superiores en Antropología Social.

Soriano, Antonio y Laure de Saint Phalle (2005). "Entrevista a Jorge Santiago Santiago. Construcción de redes en la economía solidaria." *Revista Chimères*. No. 60, Spring 2006. Accessed via <http://www.sjsocial.org/crt/articulos/759jorge_santiago.htm>.

Subcomandante Insurgente Marcos (1997). *Siete piezas sueltas del rompecabezas mundial*, Ediciones del Frente zapatista de Liberación Nacional.

Subcomandante Insurgente Marcos (2003). *La treceava estela*. Chiapas, México.

Subcomandante Insurgente Marcos (2008). "La solidaridad como hermandad o como usura." *Revista Rebeldía*. No. 57, Year 5, p. 4, January.

Vasílievich Ilienkov, Évald (1975). "Elevarse de lo abstracto a lo concreto." *El capital, teoría, estructura y método*, Tomo I, México: Ediciones de Cultura popular.

Wallerstein, Immanuel (2003). *Después del liberalismo*. México: Siglo XXI.

Womack Jr., John (2009). *Rebelión en Chiapas: Una ontología histórica*. México.

Zamora Lomelí, Carla Beatriz (2010). "Conflicto y violencia entre el Estado y los actores colectivos. Un estudio de caso: El Frente de pueblos en Defensa de la Tierra en San Salvador Atenco, Estado de México, 2001-2009." Tesis, México: El Colegio de México.

Websites

http://es.wikipedia.org/wiki/Convenci%C3%B3n_Nacional_ Democr%C3%A1tica

http://our-global-u.org/oguorg/

http://palabra.ezln.org.mx/comunicados/1994/1994_06_10_d.htm http://palabra.ezln.org.mx/comunicados/1995/1995_01_01_a.htm http://palabra.ezln.org.mx/comunicados/1998/1998_07_a.htm http://www.coloquiointernacionalandresaubry.org/

http://www.madera1965.com.mx/

http://zapateando.wordpress.com/2011/09/22

http://pglobal.org

www.autonomiazapatista.com

www.economiasolidaria.net

www.ecosol.org.br

www.laneta.org/desmiac/index.html

www.reasnet.com

www.redescolombia.com

www.riless.ungs.edu.ar

www.ripess.net

www.sipaz.org

www.vidadigna.info

CPSIA information can be obtained
at www.ICGtesting.com
Printed in the USA
LVHW071500080422
715712LV00006B/245

9 781662 918049